# PRINCESSES

# Princesses

BY CHRISTINE LEVITE
AND JULIE MOLINE

FRANKLIN WATTS
NEW YORK ✳ LONDON ✳ TORONTO ✳ SYDNEY
1989

Photographs are courtesy of: Penguin Photo: p. 101; UPI/
Bettmann: pp. 102, 111, 113, 114, 123, 126, 130, 131, 139, 143, 149;
Gamma/Liaison: pp. 103 (Photo Reporters), 106 (Giribaldi),
107 (Gilberte Tourte), 108, 112 (F. Apesteguy), 132 (Shelley
Spooner), 133 (G. de Keerle/Spooner Pictures), 134 and 135
(Michael Soulsby/Spooner), 136 (Desmond O'Neil/Spooner);
Pictorial Parade: pp. 104 (Imapress), 105 (AGIP), 109 (D.R.),
110 (AGIP/Robert Cohn), 115, 116, 117; The Norwegian Infor-
mation Service in the U.S.: pp. 118, 119; Photoreporters: pp.
120, 121, 122 (N.T.B./Bjorn Sigurdson), 144 (Werner Baum),
145 (Doug Vann); Information Department, Embassy of
Spain: p. 142; Pictorial Parade: pp. 124 (Popperfoto), 125
(Tim Boxer), 127, 128, 129 (Central Press), 137 (Independent
Television News), 138, 140, 141 (London Daily Express), 147,
148 (Darlene Hammond); Sygma: p. 146 (H. Newton).

Library of Congress Cataloging-in-Publication Data
Levite, Christine.
    Princesses / by Christine Levite and Julie Moline.
      p.   cm.
    Bibliography: p.
    Includes index.
    Summary: Brief biographies of eleven modern princesses, one from
Africa, one from Iran, and nine from western Europe.
    ISBN 0-531-10772-8
    1. Europe—Princes and princesses—Biography—Juvenile literature.
    2. Princesses—Biography—Juvenile literature.  [1. Princesses.]
    I. Moline, Julie.   II. Title.
    D1074.L48 1989
    940'.0992—dc20
    [B]      89-8955   CIP   AC

# CONTENTS

# PRINCESSES

# INTRODUCTION

Princesses abound throughout literature. There's the story of Cinderella, who by virtue of her beauty and modesty wins the heart of Prince Charming. There's the fable of Sleeping Beauty, who is put under a spell by a jealous witch; the princess and everyone else in her father's kingdom fall asleep for a hundred years, until a prince from a nearby kingdom breaks the spell by giving her a kiss. There's the tale of Rapunzel, who when locked in a tower in a forest is clever enough to realize that her long, golden hair makes a ladder of sorts. A handsome prince uses the hair-ladder to climb up the tower to visit her while she is imprisoned. Enchanted by her loveliness, he rescues her and marries her.

There's the amusing story of the princess and the pea, in which a young princess, lost in a storm, seeks refuge at a castle. There live a king and queen and their young prince, who is unhappy because he cannot find a suitable bride. The wet traveler, who is a stranger to them, tells her hosts that she is a real princess, but they don't believe her. Luckily, the queen knows of a way to prove the girl's identity. She puts a pea under a stack of twenty mattresses and insists that the girl sleep high up on the top of the pile. The queen knows that a real princess can feel the pea; a commoner cannot. Naturally, the princess tosses and turns all night. The next morning, when the queen asks how she slept, the princess replies that she couldn't sleep at all, because there was something under her bed that kept bruising her. Her real identity proven, she marries the prince and lives happily ever after.

Relying on fairy tales like these, it's easy to describe a typical princess. She's a young woman who is smart, kind, and beautiful. She attends royal balls, rides through the countryside in a gilded coach, charms everyone around her, and waits patiently for her Prince Charming to triumphantly claim her hand. The royal couple then live, as the saying goes, happily ever after.

Fairy tales are certainly fun to read and fun to think and dream about. But they're basically stories—creative works of fiction, not historical fact. Many cultures have handed down, generation after generation, the story of Cinderella, but there was no *real* Cinderella who served as the model for the story. And chances are pretty slim that any of the real princesses who lived in Cinderella's time—the Middle Ages and Renaissance—got to live happily ever after.

Life in the Middle Ages wasn't easy, even for royalty. Living conditions were uncomfortable, to say the least. Castles may be gorgeous to look at, but inside they're cold, damp, and drafty in winter and hot and stuffy in summer. In most countries, there was a constant threat of war, political uprisings, and all sorts of treachery and tyranny. In all countries, disease was a terrible reality to rich and poor alike.

In those days, unlike today, there were literally hundreds of kingdoms at any given time. Some were huge—the size of a country—and very, very rich; others were small, impoverished, and without the resources to defend against rivals and marauders. Life for a wealthy princess may have been filled with luxuries, but life for a poor one often meant living in virtual poverty. Poor princesses ate bad food, didn't have enough warm clothes, and had to work hard from dawn to dusk.

These real-life princesses often did marry princes, but the real-life princes were often less than charming. These marriages were often based more on political reasons than on love. Rulers, from ancient times up to the twentieth century, often banded together with their allies to strengthen themselves against their enemies. Their bonds were then sealed by an "arranged" marriage between their sons and daughters. This ensured peace between the families and, in some cases, kept both kingdoms' lands together. Often, these marriages were arranged even before the future bride and groom were born. And it mattered little if there were huge gaps in ages, or that the children didn't speak the same languages, or that the two hadn't met before the marriage ceremony. Princesses simply had no choice in the matter, and divorce was not an option.

In 1766, for example, Princess Caroline Matilda of Great Britain had to marry King Christian VII of Denmark. She was fifteen; he was seventeen. He may have been young, but he was mean and soon became notorious for his cruel treatment of his young bride. Eventually, he went insane; his nickname was Mad King Christian.

Princess Isabella II of Spain was thirteen and single when she officially became queen in 1843. Soon after her coronation, English, French, and Austrian rulers all began making their own suggestions concerning whom she could marry. Out of all the possibilities, there was only one prince all three rulers could agree on—Don Francisco de Asis. Unfortunately, poor Isabella found him repulsive, but she married him anyway. Needless to say it was not a happy marriage.

Other princesses throughout history have had fairy-tale-style romances that were not allowed, for various reasons, to lead to marriage. In 1890, Princess Hélène, daughter of the Compte de Paris, pretender to the French throne, fell in love with England's Duke of Clarence. The two wanted to get married, but the Catholic Compte refused to allow his daughter to change her religion. (In order to marry a member of the Protestant English royal family, she would have had to convert.)

More recently, Princess Margaret, younger sister of Queen Elizabeth, found an important relationship doomed, too, but not because of religion. Her boyfriend, a pilot and hero of World War II, Group Captain Peter Townsend, was not only a commoner (he had no royal blood) but was divorced as well. For royals, marrying a divorced person often has serious consequences; it is so frowned upon that in many royal families, members who insist on marrying someone who has been divorced must renounce their right to the throne. This often means they have to give up their yearly allowance, too, and that can be a considerable amount of money.

Although Margaret was over twenty-five at the time, and by English law could marry anyone she wanted, she chose to give up the man she loved in order to retain her link to the crown. Later Margaret married photographer Antony Armstrong-Jones, the son of the Countess of Rosse in England. They had two children, but the marriage was not a happy one, and they eventually divorced.

Crushed love affairs are distressing enough, but they seem petty compared to the true danger that many princesses have faced. Violence—and the fear of it—appears like a theme throughout the centuries. Unpopular royals have been executed, imprisoned, or sent into exile, and princesses were given no special consideration because of their sex. And whenever there is political instability or war, royal families have reason to fear for their lives.

Probably the most frightening example of recent royal tragedy was that of the family of Czar Nicholas II of Russia. Nicholas, his wife Alexandra, and their five children—Prince Alexei, and Princesses Olga, Tatiana, Maria, and Anastasia—were murdered, shot by firing squad, in 1918, shortly after the start of the Russian Revolution.

Two years later, the royal family of Hungary, which once ruled over the vast Austro-Hungarian Empire, nearly met with the same fate. After a communist government was formed in 1919, the Emperor feared that his family would be killed the way the Czar's was. The family fled to Switzerland. The youngest princess, Elisabeth, later married Prince Heinrich of Liechtenstein, and is mother of the current ruler of that tiny country.

Other royal families had to flee their war-torn countries during World War II to escape from the Nazis. The Norwegians and Swedes took refuge in England. The Belgian royal family, including Princess Josephine-Charlotte and her two brothers, fled first to France, then hid in Spain. They were caught and escorted to Germany by two hundred armed German soldiers. The three children were held captive from June 1944 to March 1945 and barely survived a long, brutal winter. Princess Josephine-Charlotte later married Umberto II, who was crowned king of Italy in 1946, but his rule only lasted one month. The Italian people had voted to discard the Royal House of Savoy.

Seeing the end of the monarchy affected many royal families around the world. Communist revolutions, government decrees, and special votes called plebescites, which occur when a country's citizens are asked by the government to choose sides on a very important issue, all led to the downfall of royal rule in Brazil, Bulgaria, Egypt, Greece, Hungary, Italy, France, Russia, Romania, Turkey, Prussia, Germany, and Yugoslavia, among others. To this day, some royals are not allowed to live in the countries their ancestors once ruled. Others, after a special "law of return" is passed, are allowed to come back. And in many countries, such as Italy, France, Brazil, and Germany, members of the royal family continue to use their royal titles, even though royalty hasn't ruled for decades.

* * *

Of course, for all their fantasy, there is some truth in fairy tales. Princesses often do end up marrying princes. Even after only a few generations, this kind of intermarrying means that a lot of royal children in different countries are actually cousins. And when these cousins marry, which often does happen, family trees begin to get very complicated!

Consider just one person on one branch of the European royal family tree: England's Queen Victoria. She had seven daughters; four of them married princes. Margaret married King Gustav VI Adolf of Sweden; Victoria married Friedrich III, German emperor and king of Prussia; Helena married Prince Christian of Schleswig-Holstein; and Beatrice married Prince Henry of Battenberg.

Queen Victoria's granddaughters also did very well with marriages to princes. Maud married Prince Charles of Denmark; Marie married Ferdinand I, king of Romania; Sophie married Constantine I, king of the Hellenes (Greece); and Ena married King Alfonso XIII of Spain. In two generations, Victoria's offspring helped interconnect seven countries!

Still, fairy tales do tend to offer a somewhat idealistic and inaccurate picture of royal life. Rare is the story in which the good princess becomes anything more than a helpmate to the prince or king she married. And there have been plenty of cases of bad princesses—spoiled, rude, stupid, or merely comical. Princess Catherine of Wurttemberg, for instance, was famous for being fat and wearing clothes that matched her purple face. So it would seem, judging from these stories, that the only role a princess could play was behind the scenes, with little function other than ensuring that a future generation of royalty was born.

In real life, many princesses, in fact, grew up to be quite powerful. Some were very influential in their father's or brother's or husband's courts. And there are many cases of princesses who grew up to assume the throne. In doing so, they were able to greatly affect the course of history.

In sixteenth-century England, two daughters of King Henry VIII became queen of England: Mary Tudor also known as Bloody Mary because of the brutality which occured under her reign, ruled from 1553 until 1558. Her half-sister Elizabeth succeeded her and ruled until her death in 1603. Several generations later, Anne, daughter of King James II, ruled Great Britain from 1702–1714.

It wasn't until the nineteenth century that another country's princess would inherit the throne.

In Spain, there was a special vote allowing Princess Isabella II to begin her reign after her father's death in 1833. She ruled until 1868, when she was overthrown. Isabella was forced to live in exile until her death in 1904, because she was forbidden to return to her country.

The twentieth century has seen the greatest number of female rulers, all of whom began their lives as princesses: Queen Victoria of England, who died in 1901; her granddaughter, the current queen, Elizabeth II; Queen Juliana of the Netherlands, who abdicated (voluntarily gave up the throne) in 1980 so that her daughter, Princess Beatrix, could assume it; and the current queen of Denmark, Margrethe, who is the first female ruler in the history of her country. Until she assumed power, there had been a long line of alternating King Frederiks and King Christians since 1513.

The twentieth century has seen more change than all centuries preceding it, combined. So it may seem odd that an ancient tradition like monarchy can survive well into such a modern age. It's true that many countries have chosen to replace kings and queens with different forms of government—some socialist, others democratic. At the same time, in countries where a monarchy still exists the royal family has never been more popular. There are even people in the United States who'd like to see a monarchy established here!

The lives of princesses in any age are fascinating, but you might be particularly curious to see what the life of a modern-day princess is like. Is being a princess a blessing or a burden? Is it anything like what it was like fifty, a hundred years ago, or more? Do princesses wish they could trade places, even for a little while, with "regular" women? How do they spend their days? Are they free to do exactly as they please—all the time? Can they marry someone other than a prince? What do they worry about? How do they feel about all the press coverage they get, and the lack of privacy? In general, how are their hopes and dreams different from those of ordinary people?

In the following chapters eleven princesses from eight royal families are profiled. With the exception of Princess Elizabeth of Toro, who is forty-seven, all were under the age of thirty-nine when this book was written. Some are married with children; others are still in high school. Some were born princesses and know only of a life that's been dominated by their royal status. Others have married into royal families and have had to learn to adjust to life in a royal family and to life in the spotlight.

All these girls and women have something in common—their title—but their personalities and their lifestyles vary dramatically.

# PRINCESS CAROLINE
# AND PRINCESS STEPHANIE
# OF MONACO

Monaco is a tiny country—one of the smallest in the world—but it attracts a tremendous amount of attention. The principality is known for its stunning setting overlooking the Mediterranean Sea, its casino nightlife that attracts big spenders, and its fascinating royal family.

His Serene Highness Prince Rainier III governs this pretty spot of land in the southeast corner of France. He is the royal sovereign, or ruler, of about 30,000 people, and, since Monaco is a constitutional monarchy, he has more actual power than Britain's Queen Elizabeth with her 900 million subjects.

Prince Rainier is also the father of two strong-minded daughters. While he has been able to turn Monaco into a major center for tourists and has fought off attempts to weaken his political power, he has often had a hard time with his girls as they've grown up.

Both Princess Caroline, the eldest child of the family and Princess Stephanie, the youngest of Prince Rainier's three children, have rebelled at times against the usual image people have of the "perfect little princesses." They've done what they wanted, sometimes to the dismay of their parents and Monaco, in trying to find their own definitions of how a princess should act. And, as their stories show, the young women, as they've grown up, have become talented individuals as well as responsible royals.

* * *

From the moment she was born, Princess Caroline of Monaco captured the world's attention. Church bells rang to celebrate the event, a twenty-one gun salute shook the land, and there was dancing in the streets. The palace celebrated with champagne for everyone in Monte Carlo.

This was, after all, the first child of a handsome prince and his stunning wife, the American movie star Grace Kelly. And their home was a grand palace in a tiny Mediterranean principality known for attracting the rich and famous.

As she's grown from little ballerina to sophisticated lady, Caroline has found her own way, despite all the attention and distractions. She has, in fact, learned how to live in the spotlight.

Rebellious when younger, Caroline has blossomed into the model of a princess. She's the mother of three children and works hard to promote the arts in her country. But the maturity has come with its heartaches, too. Her mother was killed in a car accident when Caroline was twenty-five. Since that time, she has had to serve as "First Lady" of Monaco, fulfilling the many duties that were carried out by Princess Grace. Caroline also suffered through an unhappy first marriage before settling into a happier relationship with Stefano Casiraghi, the Italian businessman she married in 1983.

The story of Princess Caroline's life is dramatic, and it proves that a royal heritage doesn't help anyone escape the pangs of growing up.

Caroline Louise Marguerite was born on January 23, 1957, and immediately became the "heiress presumptive," the one who would inherit the throne of Monaco from her father, Prince Rainier III of the House of Grimaldi. Only fourteen months later, however, her brother, Albert, arrived on the scene. Heralded by a 101-gun salute, Albert became the new heir apparent, the child who would eventually rule the country. Prince Rainier made Caroline curtsy to her little brother, which no doubt made her a little jealous of Albert. Her sister, Princess Stephanie, was born in 1965, and the three children grew up in a 180-room castle with each other as playmates. Caroline often acted the part of the bossy older sister.

Her early years made her a bit of a loner, she now recalls. "I've always felt that when I had a problem I could find the solution within myself," she said. "Maybe that's because I grew up in a special atmosphere, which meant that I did spend an awful lot of time alone as a child."

Caroline was tutored at the palace until she was eight, and little girls had to be brought in for play times. Understandably, she felt different from her playmates, and she usually wanted to have the last word. True to her independent spirit, Caroline was not a sweet, lovable youngster. "I was the most horrible child. I never wanted to sit on anybody's lap, including my mother's. I was always squirming out of people's arms." Although she says she's very affectionate with her own children, she still doesn't like to be "fussed over or waited on."

Princess Grace tried to make her children familiar with American ways as they were being raised in this privileged household. Grace was a young movie actress from Philadelphia when she married her fairy-tale prince. The two had a brief and formal courtship. After they'd met only once, Rainier visited Philadelphia and brought with him an engagement ring. When Grace accepted his proposal, she also accepted his attitude about the new role she should play. Specifically, she agreed to abandon her career as an actress—princesses didn't work, after all—and devote herself to Monaco. She had to make a choice between personal ambition and married life, since women in the 1950s were expected to be content with being a wife and mother. The restriction seems all the more old-fashioned when compared to the way Caroline and Stephanie have pursued their dreams.

If Grace Kelly ever objected, however, she never admitted this in public, although there were times in which she'd perform on stage for charity audiences. She also remained friends with the show business people she knew, making frequent visits to the United States.

For a few years, Caroline and her sister went to summer camp with their American cousins in the mountains of Pennsylvania. The family also vacationed in Hollywood and on Cape Cod. Like many girls, Caroline and Stephanie took ballet, swimming, tennis, horseback riding, piano, and flute lessons after school. Caroline attended class at the local Catholic girls' school, learning to speak Italian, German, and Spanish in addition to her parents' languages of English and French.

The royal family lived at the palace during the week and visited their retreat, Roc Agel, on weekends and during the summer. At this old farmhouse in the mountains above the city of Monte Carlo, the children could tend to their horses, ponies, goats, cows, and rabbits.

When she was fourteen, Caroline was sent to St. Mary's, a Catholic boarding school in England. Her parents felt she needed a more strict environment, away from the fun-loving atmosphere of Monaco. The new school did not stop Caroline from loving the party life, however. She had the beauty and the social position to attract a lot of boys, and Caroline made the most of it.

After finishing high school, Caroline enrolled at the Sorbonne in Paris. She eventually got a degree in philosophy and child psychology, even though she was seen more frequently in nightclubs than on campus. Her mother spent much of her time in Paris then in order to keep a closer eye on her strong-willed daughter, but Princess Grace's scoldings did little to change Caroline.

At one of those Parisian discos, Caroline, then nineteen, met Philippe Junot, a reported "playboy" who was seventeen years older than her. The young princess was swept away by Junot and his attitude of not caring one bit about her royal background. Months later, in early 1977, he proposed and she accepted, only to find her parents very much against the union. Junot was no aristocrat, he had no real career, and Caroline seemed more in love with him than he was with her. The Rainiers, expecting Caroline to be sensible, demanded that she wait at least one year before marrying.

After nearly a year of being engaged, the twenty-one-year-old Caroline went ahead and married her first love on June 29, 1978, despite her parent's disapproval. The couple set up housekeeping in a Paris penthouse and visited Monaco frequently, with Caroline keeping up her duties in charity work there.

Two years after their wedding, however, Caroline returned home to stay. The marriage had fallen apart. Hurt and humbled, she came back to the support of her family. A legal divorce followed, but her mother was not able to convince the Vatican, which oversees the Catholic church's approval of divorce, to grant her daughter an annulment—the procedure that would allow her to marry again with the blessing of the church.

For the next two years, Princess Caroline seemed aimless as she mixed with the glamorous jet-set crowd that gathers in Monaco. She appeared as a beautiful, rich-and-famous divorcée, dating celebrities and having well-publicized romantic flings. She wrote in her diary at that time: "I do not think I am the ideal woman for a man—with my tormented past, my uncertain present, and perhaps my melancholy future."[1] These sad predictions were written shortly before the tragedy that would alter her life.

On September 13, 1982, Princess Grace, driving Stephanie back to Monaco from Roc Angel, lost control of her car on the twisty road and suffered injuries in the crash that would lead to her death a few days later. Caroline, who was out of town when she received word of the accident, rushed back to Monaco and was the strength of the family during the aftermath. She was the one who made the decisions about the funeral, and she stood by her grieving father and stunned brother in the cathedral where Rainier and Grace had been married and the children had all been baptized. Stephanie was still recovering from her injuries at the time of the funeral, and it was a somber Caroline who tried to comfort her father, the monarch.

To everyone's surprise, Caroline, when faced with this crisis, became the anchor for her family. After a period of mourning, she went to benefits that Grace had been scheduled to attend, accompanying her father to the annual Red Cross Ball, *the* social event in Monaco, and, wearing a Scout uniform, taking the local Girl Guides on a camping trip to the Grimaldi estate near Paris.

Very suddenly, Caroline felt that her place was to represent her country, to carry on with dignity the example of her mother, who had become a beloved figure among the Monegasque. Caroline served as president of the Princess Grace Foundation, which is dedicated to promote the arts, and headed the Monaco Garden Club as well as the committee that sponsors springtime arts festivals.

She also kept in operation a crisis hot-line for troubled teens, a project she'd founded two years before. She took steps, too, to realize her mother's dream of recreating a ballet troupe in Monaco. This most ambitious project took three years to complete. In December 1985, the Ballets de Monte Carlo made its debut in the newly restored Opera House. Thus, Caroline finished the work that her mother began. The young princess hopes to make Monte Carlo an international dance capital.

Dedicating herself to these efforts on behalf of Monaco gave Caroline a new focus in life. No longer rebelling, she became calmer and more confident, though obviously saddened by the sorrowful experiences of her mother's death and her own divorce.

In July 1983, a new man entered her life. He was Stefano Casiraghi, who is three-and-one-half years younger than Caroline. The son of a wealthy Italian industrialist, he is described as thoughtful, hardworking, refined, and smart. Casiraghi seemed to be a better partner for the Princess than Junot had been. He had already built a business in import/export and construction and could not have been accused of seeking his fortune through royal marriage.

The Vatican's decision not to grant Caroline an annulment meant that she could not marry in the church. So, the two were married in a fifteen-minute civil ceremony in December 1983.

The next summer, Caroline gave birth to a son, Andrea Albert Casiraghi. Two years later, in August 1986, a daughter was born, named Charlotte Marie Pomeline, after Prince Rainier's mother. In September 1987, the couple had a second son, Pierre.

For Princess Caroline, life is simpler now. The family lives in a spacious villa, Le Clos St. Pierre, that is only a three-minute walk from the pink and white royal palace.

Stefano escorts his wife to galas, but the two lead separate lives during the day. He spends twelve hours a day running his enterprises, while Caroline has her office at the palace and usually works from 10:30 A.M. until 5:00 P.M. on her official duties. In contrast to her Paris years, she prefers to be in bed early these days.

Everyday life for Princess Caroline involves serving the people of Monaco. She lends her name, as honorary president, to such groups as the Girl Guides and the Ladies' Needle and Thread Society, a women's club. Despite all this time spent on good works, Caroline frowns if anyone calls her Monaco's First Lady, since she feels that she's not that different from other women. "I work for my country as everyone else here works. If I can do something in an area I know a bit about, that's very well. In the end, it's a job like any other."[2] And the tourist mecca of Monaco, the Mediterranean playground, is not that different from the rest of the world. "It is home rather than a fantasy-land in a travel brochure, and I lead the active life of a working mother."[3]

Motherhood brings her a lot of satisfaction. She often brings one or two of her children with her to the office, and although she has two nannies who help with the toddlers, Caroline likes to bathe the children and fix their meals.

Those who meet her for the first time comment that Caroline has a natural warmth. She dresses elegantly, but she is not very concerned about presenting herself as a glittering member of royalty. In private moments, the statuesque princess (she's five feet, eight-and-one-half-inches [176 cm] tall) likes to dress casually and go without makeup, often pulling her dark brown hair into a pony tail.

Calling herself a romantic, Caroline writes poems and keeps a journal. She has also written articles for magazines based on interviews with other famous people. Regarding this thoughtful part of her personality, she admits being a little impatient. "I'm an Aquarian. They're restless. They want something new all the time. I hate monotony, everyday plans and schedules. I need time alone for reflection and solitude. I like to be alone a lot."[4] She claims that the Pisces sign also fits her. "Pisces are sedate, quiet, reasonable people who tend to avoid conflict. So I think that plays an important part in my life and relationships."[5]

With so much of her day spent on official duties, Caroline says she needs to guard her private life from public view. She intends to raise her children with as little publicity and royal fuss as possible.

Caroline has always loved ballet and music. She studied dancing for ten years, and she became an excellent flutist. Her other passion is skiing, and the Casiraghi family likes nothing better than to go to St. Moritz for a "real vacation" every February. The children are learning the finer points of skiing from their expert parents. The Casiraghis own apartments in Paris and Milan and houses in Como (in northern Italy) and St. Moritz.

What role Princess Caroline plays in the future of Monaco will depend on her father . . . and her brother. Prince Rainier announced in 1988 that his son will inherit the throne, laying to rest rumors that Caroline would be named to succeed her father. If Prince Albert marries, in all likelihood, Caroline's power will decrease.

With a fierce determination that's now under control, Princess Caroline has become committed to the Monaco cause—for whatever happens. "Ten years from now, perhaps with a few more children, I hope I will still be active in keeping Monaco exciting," she said in 1988.[6]

In the meantime, she will be a strong, involved mother trying to raise a normal family as she performs her public duties. But her children, unlike Caroline, have no royal claim. They're simply Casiraghis, and when she tells them bedtime stories, she says, there are no kings or queens, princes or princesses in the tales. The make-believe involves ordinary boys and girls, and the endings are always happy ones.

* * *

When you're young, beautiful, and talented, life is a fast-spinning merry-go-round. And, when you happen to be a princess on top of everything else, the world watches your every turn on the carousel.

Princess Stephanie of Monaco could be seen as taking a wild ride as she tests her skills in different careers, enjoys the privileged life of a Monaco royal, and skips from romance to romance. The youngest child of Prince Rainier III and Princess Grace, Stephanie has taken over the position once occupied by her older sister, Caroline, that of family rebel.

An independent attitude may run in the family, but Princess Stephanie is intent on expressing herself as an individual. She has shown that no matter how palace officials or news magazines express their shock at her youthful escapades, she is going to set her own style for what a princess can do.

She is sometimes described as having a "Mediterranean personality." In contrast to her mother, who was cooly refined—a model of perfection—Stephanie, like her sister, has a fiery personality and a zest for excitement. She's emotional, both in the

ventures as with her wild, high-spirited lifestyle. The all-night partying became noticeable when Stephanie had to be hospitalized for a week for exhaustion.

On her part, Stephanie said later that *she* had become dissatisfied with modeling, even though she was being offered fees of $10,000 per session. "I didn't like it anymore. I gave it up,"[3] she said without explaining her reasons. She quickly found a new creative path. She got a position as an apprentice at the Dior fashion salon in Paris, where high-fashion clothes are created for the world's wealthiest women. But after less than a year as an assistant there, Stephanie had other ideas.

At Dior, she had designed bathing suits with Alix de la Comble. In November 1984, Stephanie showed Alix a new and different suit design, and the two decided to start their own business, specializing in bathing suits. Financed by loans from each of their brothers, the women set up a one-room shop. The design firm was called Pool Position and featured suits in the $80 to $150 price range.

Stephanie, a real water lover, saw the need for her product. At her first showing, she said, "I've lived for over twenty years on the edge of the sea without ever managing to find shops with swimsuits that really pleased me."[4]

With her whole family watching, Stephanie was the backstage star of the show when the swimwear line debuted in Monaco in 1985. Fashion experts praised the colorful, sleek, and sexy suits. And after the last model walked the "runway," which was around a swimming pool, Stephanie and Alix took their bows and then jumped into the pool as the crowd applauded. Even Papa Rainier, who admitted to being a bit nervous about his daughter's business, cheered proudly. In less than a year, Pool Position had sold about 28,000 swimsuits, and the operation continues to be successful.

In 1985 and 1986, Stephanie worked hard to promote her fashions, making appearances in Europe and the United States. But celebrity-watchers didn't think of her as a serious businesswoman. Instead, the press covered her successes and failures with a series of boyfriends—some famous, such as movie star Rob Lowe, and most considered by high society to be way below her status. News of her dating and partying made all the papers.

Her whirlwind life-style usually included regular stops at the chic nightspots in Monaco, where she'd sip champagne and dance until 5:00 A.M. Daytime was spent on the beach. Stephanie's every action—whether it be playing pranks like stuffing a waiter's pockets with ice cubes or suntanning topless—would be recorded in the next day's papers, so that everyone had the details of her private life, with pictures to match.

Stephanie's two-month romance with Rob Lowe didn't come about through friends or a party. They learned of each other through a television program. During a guest spot on the "Tonight" show, Lowe revealed that Princess Stephanie was his fantasy date. In response, she told the French magazine *Globe* that she thought Rob was just about perfect too. Hollywood took it from there. A press agent for Lowe's movie studio acted as matchmaker, and the two had a fling that fueled rumors internationally. Was Lowe going to be the chosen one for Stephanie? Hardly. Their dating on both continents at the most glamourous of parties quickly became history. Stephanie was off with someone new—a Los Angeles nightclub owner. When this romance ended after two years, Rainier was much relieved.

Reports of her social life made all the papers, and the world could have concluded that this youngest member of the royal family was wild and troubled, the victim of wealth and of trauma stemming from her mother's death. In Monaco, however, people were not so quick to condemn her. They thought she acted like most kids her age. "We're proud of both her success and her spirit," said one government official.[5]

Stephanie surprised everyone again in 1986 by taking an altogether different direction. She recorded an album of pop songs, most of them ballads. The album, *Besoin* (Need), hit the top of the charts in France and West Germany.

Her new career demanded that she promote herself as a rock star which meant traveling by private plane with a group of employees and friends. On the insistence of her father, she is now accompanied by an ever-watchful bodyguard and a team that includes a hairdresser, a press aide, a personal secretary, and a representative from the record company. A bit spoiled as a youngster, Stephanie usually likes to have people cater to her, to help her deal with the duties of being both a budding singer and a blossoming princess.

"Live Your Life" was the one of the most popular songs on her first album, but the tune "Flash" almost sums up her frantic jump into adulthood. The lyrics are, "Flash for love. Flash for life. It works or it breaks."

Having a long list of ex-boyfriends by the time she was twenty-three, Stephanie said then that she felt many men only wanted to be with her because of her fame, her star status, or even the fortune of her family. "I was fooled several times when I was younger. You learn by experience, and not all experiences are fun."[6] She had been hurt by false people, she said.

Stephanie once described the type of person who could make her happy. "Looks—I don't really care. I don't have a special kind of man, a type. It depends on what is inside. He has to be funny, a great sense of humor."[7] He would also have to be an equal match for her. "I love life, and I enjoy life! I have fun, cracking jokes and doing crazy things. He has to have the same kind of mind as me. And, he has to be very honest, sincere, and sensitive."

Princess Stephanie is speaking very differently about her goals in life, however. "I envy my sister and wish that I were going home to a husband and children,"[8] she said in the spring of 1987, after Caroline announced that she was pregnant with her third child.

In August 1988, Stephanie announced that she'd found a new man in her life: her manager, Ron Bloom. At last report, the two were discussing marriage, but Bloom, who is Jewish, was asked to convert to Stephanie's faith, Catholicism, and Prince Rainer had yet to give his opinion about the matter.

As determined as Stephanie is to have fun with the people of *her* choice, the princess maintains a deep love and respect for her father and for her royal legacy.

When asked if Prince Rainier disapproved of her singing career, Stephanie was firm. "Believe me, if my father did not like it, I would not do it. My father knows that I have to have my own experiences to find out what is good for me. And he trusts me. When he calls, I'm right there. I never forget that I'm a princess of my country."[9]

In many ways, Stephanie has found a balance in her spin at life. She is still involved with the swimsuit business; she is working on her singing and sitting still for the interviews that will help promote her records, and she is an active participant in Monaco's many charity events.

Stephanie is learning that she has skills that stand alone. She also is mature enough to realize, "The fact that I was born famous helps me a lot."[10]

Fame hasn't made her helpless. Besides having fresh good looks, a singing voice, and an eye for clothes, this princess can cook, having been taught the finer points of kitchen work by her mother. Stephanie has no patience with rich girls who "don't know how to wash the dishes or boil water."[11]

Royal or not, young women need to take care of themselves, she believes. "If something happens, what are they going to do? I know that I'll always be able to get along in life!"[12]

She also insists that all the attention is not going to change her. "My head will never swell up. I always will stay the same."[13] Stay the same? Not a chance.

## PRINCESS ELIZABETH
## OF TORO

Most of the world's princesses have grown up in European capitals and spent their adult lives attending ceremonies and parties to fulfill their official duties. But Princess Elizabeth Bagaaya Nyabongo was raised as a member of the royal house of Toro in the African country of Uganda, the eldest child of the king of the Batoro tribe, and her life story is one of hardship and fierce dedication.

Although she was born an African princess, Elizabeth saw her royal standing disappear when her country became a democratic nation. Now, after years of struggling under the less than democratic governments that controlled the nation until a few years ago, Princess Elizabeth is serving as a diplomat, working in Washington, D.C. as a representative of the African people.

Unlike other royal women, Elizabeth of Toro has had much experience of life beyond the palace gates. She was educated at Cambridge University in England and became the first African woman to practice law in Uganda. A beautiful, tall woman with a dramatic face, she modeled for fashion magazines during one period in her life—the picture of a stylish, contemporary princess. But her background also includes many crises. She was forced to flee Uganda several times because of political clashes with its dictators, who were powerful and violent men. She withstood the scandal of being labeled an enemy of the people by these men. Yet throughout her life, Elizabeth has maintained a strong passion for the country of her birth and its struggle for stability.

When Princess Elizabeth was born in 1941, Uganda was a colony governed by Great Britain. Although united under the British Commonwealth, the four provinces of Uganda (Toro being one of them) still retained their monarchies. Elizabeth's father, the king of Toro, lived in regal comfort in a handsome palace with his family of five wives and many children.

Elizabeth had a special position—she was the first daughter of the king's first wife. In recalling her early years, she has happy memories of her home and the connection that existed between the royal family and the citizens of the land. Privileges and responsibility went hand in hand, she recalls. "We were brought up never, never to act in any way that you're superior because you are a princess. You were brought up to think that that meant to serve the people. And, the more humble you were, I think, the more people glorified you. And to do otherwise was the height of bad manners."[1]

She remembers her father as a leader who kept the palace open to the people. "Anybody could walk up here and demand audience with the king. From morning until he went to bed, this place was accessible to the entire country."[2]

At fourteen, Elizabeth was sent to England to continue her education. She attended Cambridge University, one of Britain's foremost colleges, and graduated in 1962—the same year that Uganda won its independence from Great Britain. After receiving a law degree at Cambridge, Princess Elizabeth Bagaaya returned to Uganda with the distinction of being the first African woman to be admitted to the English bar.

Her plans to practice law in Uganda ended suddenly, however. Milton Obote, who was now ruling the country with little concern for tradition or the people's will, abolished the monarchies. Princess Elizabeth was no longer accorded the rights of royalty. For a while, she worked as a lawyer in Kampala, the capital city. But the political situation worsened, and Obote's brutal police squad was allowed to arrest—or even kill—people who were suspected of disloyalty to his regime. "To be seen speaking to a princess or to be friendly to a princess was enough for you to be penalized," Elizabeth said of this period.[3]

In 1967, the terror and tension became so great that Princess Elizabeth fled to London. This would be the first of three times she would have to seek exile in another country.

While in England, Elizabeth was a sought-after guest, and at one charity fashion show, she was persuaded to model. The appearance caught the attention of the fashion world. *Vogue* featured her as a model, and she was one of the first black women to be on the cover of *Harper's Bazaar*.

In Uganda, the political unrest grew, and in 1971 Milton Obote's government was overthrown by Idi Amin, a clownish, uneducated man who was, at first, welcomed by the Ugandan people. With hopes that Amin would be a fair leader, Elizabeth gladly returned home to try to help the new government.

Amin asked her to be his roving ambassador and then named her his foreign minister in 1973. During the time she held this position, Princess Elizabeth drew comment by being outspoken on African nationalism. In a presentation to the United Nations, she argued that the African countries should be free to govern themselves without interference from other countries.

Aside from her intelligent, sharp speaking manner, she was known for her startling appearance. She wore hairdos of tight braids, heavy gold necklaces, and flowing native dresses. This made her an exotic figure among the dark-suited diplomats. They did, however, listen to her opinions, which showed that she was both well educated and fiercely committed to her country.

It became clear, though, that Idi Amin, like Obote, was compelled to react violently. Cabinet ministers who disagreed with him were found mysteriously murdered, and after ten months as a member of his government, Elizabeth was herself a victim of Amin's wrath. She had crossed him by speaking her mind about injustice and by reportedly turning down his marriage proposal.

Amin had a false report published about the princess having a love affair with a white man in Paris and having contacts with British and American spies. The dictator had Elizabeth put under house arrest but was forced to release her when other countries protested strongly.

Amin's attempts to disgrace her didn't end, however. He had the Ugandan television station broadcast pictures of a nude woman and identified her incorrectly as Princess Elizabeth. Later, she won a lawsuit against the European paper that first printed the phony pictures. To escape the persecution, Elizabeth hid in the house of a relative in Kampala while her friends arranged for her escape to Kenya, a country bordering Uganda.

Elizabeth used a disguise—masquerading as a pregnant woman—to walk across the border. "Here, modeling really helped me," she said, pointing to the fact that she knew how to use makeup to change her looks.[4] She said of that period: "I was lucky to get out. Many, many people died."[5] Some people criticized Princess Elizabeth for agreeing to be part of Amin's government, despite the fact that she was driven out. "I did not work for Amin," she stated. "I worked for Uganda."

Elizabeth was still in exile when Idi Amin was overthrown in 1979. Unfortunately, the former strong-man Milton Obote came back to run the country. It was at this point, as the country trembled in fear of its first dictator, that Princess Elizabeth became a rebel. Working in London as a lawyer, she became a spokesperson for the National Resistance Movement, a group that wanted to bring a more democratic system to Uganda. In 1981, she married Wilbur Nyabongo, an engineer who was very active in the resistance movement as well, and the couple spent much of their time seeking support for political change in Uganda.

Meanwhile, outside the capital of Kampala, Ugandans suspected of disloyalty to Obote were being killed; an estimated 300,000 people were murdered between 1981 and 1986.

During her time in London, Princess Elizabeth traveled to different countries to speak about the Ugandan struggle. She also found time to write an autobiography, entitled *African Princess,* and to act in a few films, including the movie *Sheena.*

The leader of the resistance movement was Yoweri Museveni, and, in 1986, it was Museveni who took power when Obote was overthrown. He vowed to restore human rights and to bring more stability to the country. Soon afterwards, Princess Elizabeth was again asked by her nation's leader to play an active part in government, and in 1986, she became Uganda's Ambassador to the United States. She accepted with enthusiasm. She presented herself to President Reagan, took a first look at the Washington, D.C., embassy building that would be her headquarters, and prepared for the move that she and her husband would make to the United States.

What should have been a triumphal return to public life was jarred by tragedy. While Elizabeth was flying to Uganda to attend her brother's wedding, her husband, who was to join her there, crashed in a plane he was copiloting. Distraught over his death, Elizabeth vowed at the time: "I will never remarry."[6]

After two months of mourning, Princess Elizabeth threw herself into her new diplomatic duties, which included restoring the embassy and rebuilding the country's reputation and ties to the rest of the world.

For the first task, the princess was not above playing Cinderella. The embassy, which had become very run down, needed to be scrubbed and repainted so that it could operate as a proper place for business. Despite her regal background, Elizabeth set a firm policy against expensive touches. The building's reconstruction was done on a budget, and there were to be no lavish parties or limousines.

The flamboyance she had shown when she was a diplomat under Amin's rule was gone. Her main mission was to show that Uganda was now a maturing country, able to govern itself in a more democratic way.

As an ambassador, Elizabeth has tried to encourage trade between the United States and

Uganda—the African country relies heavily on the United States buying coffee beans, Uganda's main export. She has also urged American companies to invest in Uganda by supplying better technology, training programs, and equipment so that industry there can progress. She persuaded a team of bankers to grant loans to Uganda, and this financial help is expected to allow African businesses to train employees and expand operations.

Personally, Princess Elizabeth of Toro has changed her priorities as a result of all she's been through. Instead of the intricate hairdos and gold chains, she prefers to dress simply and be as private as possible. Her hair is cropped short, and she wears little jewelry with her simple but elegant wardrobe. She insists that this is the time for hard work for herself and the citizens of Uganda in order to signal that the country values its independence.

When she returns to Toro for visits, she is greeted warmly by her family and neighbors. She no longer is treated like a princess, but she is deeply respected as a civil servant, working for the government in the best way she can.

For her, royal life is a fuzzy girlhood memory, but she can take pride in her adult accomplishments. She survived the violence of two dictators; she became a role model for African women by becoming a lawyer and returning to her native land; she made the African look fashionable through her modeling and film work, and she gained new respect for Uganda by being an intelligent ambassador.

Entangled in the political life of her nation's struggle, Princess Elizabeth of Toro considers her responsibility now to be no different from that of the people who once were her subjects. She, like others who suffered for the country, is happy to have a chance to make Uganda stronger.

"I lived in exile, and now I know I can come home, and I'm not regarded with resentment because I was a member of the royal family. I am participating in the destiny of Uganda like any other Ugandan."[7]

## PRINCESS MARTHA LOUISE
## OF NORWAY

Every May 17th, thousands of school children in Norway march through the streets of Oslo in a spirited parade. Norwegian Constitution Day, like the Fourth of July, is a time for eating ice cream and waving the flag. It's also the day that the country honors its royalty.

Every year, Princess Martha Louise and her whole family stand for hours on the balcony of the royal palace to greet the parading children, who wave up at the princess from the street. All Norwegians, after all, have the right to speak to the monarch and other members of royalty. The cheers she hears come from citizens who appreciate the ways in which these royal representatives—her grandfather, King Olav V, his children, and grandchildren—set an example of national pride for the rest of the population.

Unlike many other European countries, where kings and queens have ruled continuously for hundreds of years, Norway adopted its monarchy only in this century. The Norwegians can trace their kings back to Viking days, but their present king was born in England. His father was Danish, and his mother British. Possibly because the Norwegians chose to have a royal house, the citizens hold a special feeling for the king's family.

Martha Louise is a princess who will never be a queen, and, following the standard set by her parents and grandparents, she leads a life not too different from that of other teenagers in Norway. Her younger brother, Haakon Magnus, is the heir to the throne. He will be the one to take over the monarchy after his father, Crown Prince Harald, who will inherit the throne from King Olav. Both of the young royals are growing up with an understanding of their official position in the country, but, according to reports, neither has been spoiled by the privileges.

Martha Louise was born on September 22, 1971, the first child of Prince Harald and Crown Princess Sonja. The Norwegian broadcasting company interrupted its regular program with the joyous announcement. As soon as he heard the news, King Olav V interrupted his visit to the United States to fly home to celebrate the birth. The little girl was given two names: Martha, in honor of the king's beloved wife, who was no longer living, and Louise, in honor of another ancestor, Queen Louise of Denmark.

A pretty child with brown hair, blue eyes, and fair skin, Martha Louise received not only a double name, but a double dose of Norwegian family tradition. Although her father was noble by birth, her mother was a "commoner." Sonja was a clothing designer and the daughter of a shopkeeper when she married Prince Harald in 1968. Princess Martha Louise was brought up with a strong sense of her middle class heritage in addition to her royal background.

Prince Harald and his family have lived in Skaugum, a few miles from the capital city of Oslo, since he and his wife married. The king, on the other hand, lives alone in the Royal Palace in Oslo, and it's likely that when Harald takes the throne, Martha Louise's family will move to the enormous palace in the city.

Meanwhile, home life is quite pleasant for the two royal children. Their villa, in a very hilly area, is a spacious estate surrounded by a park, playing fields, farm animals, a swimming pool, and a garden that overlooks the Oslo fjord. The house itself is a white stone building with furnishings that have come from France, Holland, and England, as well as Norway.

Princess Martha Louise has heard many stories of her royal blood and has much to be proud of in her family background. When Norway broke from its union with Sweden in 1905 (an alliance that had lasted for almost a hundred years), it looked for a member of European royalty who would agree to be its new king. Norway turned to Prince Charles of Denmark, and he came to the country with his wife, Princess Maud, and their little son, Prince Alexander.

To show their allegiance to their new home, Charles changed his name in receiving the new title. He became King Haakon VII, and two-year-old Alexander was dubbed Olav; he is now the present king.

Although they were directly related to the kings and queens of Denmark, Sweden, and Great Britain, the family could also trace its royal blood all the way back through thirty-four generations to King Harald Fair-Hair, who united Norway in A.D. 872. In the nineteenth century, Denmark's King Christian IX was nicknamed the "father-in-law of Europe" and England's Queen Victoria was called "the grandmother of Europe." These monarchs saw that their many children married into other royal families, and the modern-day Norwegian royalty, as descendents of the two, retains particularly close ties to both countries.

While the royal position in Norway carries no political power, the family played a very important part in uniting the country during and after World War II. King Haakon and his son, then Crown Prince Olav, led the Norwegian fight against Hitler's air force. Norway fell, nonetheless, under German control, and both men had to leave the country—or be killed. Working in England to support the Allies' effort, they made radio broadcasts into their homeland—messages that lifted the spirits of their countrymen in a time when they were controlled by outsiders. With no government of their own, Norwegians looked to their king and prince as symbols of their culture.

During the war, Olav's family—his wife Martha and their children, Harald and his two sisters—lived in the United States. They were invited to stay at President Roosevelt's home, Hyde Park, to wait for the fighting to be over in Europe. When victory finally came, the King, Prince Olav, and the prince's family returned home to Norway ready to rebuild the country.

Olav became the king when his father died in 1958. In the years since, he's earned the nickname, "The People's King." He has always loved meeting the everyday people, whether it be on a snowy ski trail or during one of his palace "open houses." His friendly, open attitude was one of his strengths, proving useful in solving a problem he was to have with his son. Just after Martha Louise's father—the young Prince Harald—finished his military school education, he met a pretty woman, Sonja Haraldsen, at a party. Actually, the two had seen each other before; when they were both seven years old, he had ridden through the Oslo streets with his family and she had waved at him as he passed.

As adults, the two quickly fell in love. They wanted to get married, but the prince was a nobleman, the heir apparent, and Sonja was a commoner. For nine years, Crown Prince Harald tried to convince his father and the government that only Sonja would do as his wife. Matchmakers in European society tried unsuccessfully to find a suitable royal lady, but Harald stood firm. Since that time, of course, several other kings and princes have married commoners, but in the early 1960s this was not done, even though Harald's two sisters were permitted to marry commoners.

Finally, His Majesty King Olav V persuaded the government to consent to the wedding, and, as a sign of his approval, Olav gave the bride away. The wedding, on August 29, 1968, was attended by four kings, a grand duke, and three presidents. But if it weren't for Olav's determination, the marriage would not have taken place and Martha Louise wouldn't have been born.

Like her husband, the crown princess has been a popular royal representative of Norway. A well-educated woman—she had studied in Switzerland and at Cambridge University in England—Sonja had received an arts degree in dressmaking. As first lady, she sews only for fun, spending much of her days attending art exhibitions, serving as a director of the Red Cross, and visiting homes for the underprivileged. When Princess Martha Louise was a baby, her mother established a fund in her daughter's name, granting money to those not as fortunate—the handicapped children of Norway.

Because her parents wanted the children to grow up as normally as possible, Martha Louise and Haakon Magnus were enrolled in a public school in Oslo. At home, the two have been supervised by English nannies since their births and, consequently, speak English fluently.

The family also keeps a few British traditions in their holiday celebrations. On Christmas Eve, the royal family hangs up Christmas stockings—an uncommon custom in Scandinavia, where Father Christmas is said to come through the front door, not down the chimney. Nevertheless, the king's mother, Queen Maud, liked the British version of St. Nick better, and the family has remained true to her wishes.

Whenever their school schedule allows, the young royal members accompany their parents on official and personal trips. Several times, they have visited England for the lighting of the Christmas tree that is given by the city of Oslo to London every year.

A few years ago, the family went to Denmark, to the ancestral home of the Danish royal family. At the palace, visitors would etch their names in the glass windowpanes, and Martha Louise and her brother found a familiar name in the scratchings, spotting "Maud" in one of windows. Here was a sign from a previous century.

Athletics are very important to all Norwegians, and the royal family has always enjoyed outdoor sports. Martha Louise is no exception. Like many teenage girls, she developed a love of horses, and she's now considered an excellent rider.

Boating is a passion for most members of the royal family. Norwegians live by and love the sea, and the royals usually spend summertime at one of two vacation homes on the Norwegian coast. These are simple houses, not especially fancy in any way, but they have the decided benefit of being near the shore, near the king's favorite yacht.

Martha Louise and her brother follow the example set by old King Olav. When it came to sports, the king preferred to be in the game—not sitting on the sidelines. He won an Olympic gold medal for sailing in 1928 and competed in the ski jumping event in the winter Olympics that year. On two occasions, Crown Prince Harald competed for Norway in the Olympic sailing competition.

On board the royal yacht, *Norge,* the king has explored almost every island, creek, and bay along the Norwegian coastline. He's sailed as far north as the Arctic Ocean and as far south as the Mediterranean Sea. His son still loves the sport, too, and Crown Princess Sonja, who has her own boat, often competes in local sailing regattas.

In Norway, where winters are long and the terrain is hilly, nearly every child grows up on skis. Martha Louise learned the sport when she was little, and everyone in her family avidly takes to the slopes. Her mother, in fact, is a licensed ski instructor, and she taught both of her children. Not surprisingly, winter holidays are spend at one of several chalets owned by the royal family.

Being a member of royalty is hardly one long vacation, however. The crown prince and princess work very hard at their official duties, making appearances, shaking hands, cutting ribbons, and giving speeches as if they were ordinary folk taking care of business. They have few servants and usually wear business attire. The king and the crown prince don't have uniforms or crowns, and the princesses dress nicely, but certainly not in the lavish high-style fashions that some royals wear. Martha Louise does like dresses with fine embroidery—a style that is traditional in Norway.

As Martha Louise comes of age, she, too, will be expected to help with the business of being royalty. For this, she'll earn the respect of the Norwegian people, who already love her for her common background as well as her royal blood.

## PRINCESS YASMIN
## AGA KHAN

With exceptional beauty, talent, and wealth, Princess Yasmin Aga Khan could have led the pack of glamorous jet-setters. She might have pursued a promising career as a singer, she might have followed her mother's path into movie stardom, or she might have chosen to float through life in round after round of play and parties as her father did.

The choices were limitless and, because of that fact, Princess Yasmin Aga Khan is a surprising woman. She has set aside her personal ambitions to devote her life to working for a cause: finding a cure for Alzheimer's disease, the terrible mental disorder that killed her mother, actress Rita Hayworth.

Yasmin has been a princess with a purpose that reaches beyond typical royal duties. She was raised in the United States in well-to-do but not extravagant circumstances. Despite her royal title, she had no official meeting-and-greeting responsibilities that define many young royals' schedules.

Her father was the fabulously wealthy Aly Khan, who had the princely title as likely successor to his father, the Aga Khan, spiritual head of the Muslim faith. Being a prince with no national attachments, Aly Khan lived as he pleased, roaming the world for excitement.

In the late 1940s, the prince was taken by a famous American actress, the beautiful redhead who was the sex symbol for that decade, Rita Hayworth. In the end, their romance was as bright, and as brief, as a photographer's flash. Their wedding day in 1949 was the media event of the season, setting a certain standard for lavishness that awed even their international celebrity guests. Held at an estate on the French Riviera, the wedding reception was set around a swimming pool that was filled with 200 gallons (760 l) of perfume and festooned with floating flowers in the shape of the couple's monogram. A violin orchestra, playing on the rooftop of the home, overlooked the guests as they consumed 600 bottles of champagne and a 120-pound (54 kg) wedding cake.

The bridegroom, after all, was one of the richest men in the world and a renowned playboy; the bride was one of the most popular stars in Hollywood. Rita's wedding presents included a fabulous diamond ring and bracelet with matching earrings and hair comb, a sports car, and a race horse—racing being Aly Khan's central interest. At the Muslim ceremony that followed, a Pakistani leader declared that any children born of this union would be "soldiers of Islam."

Late in 1949, an army of reporters waited for hours outside a Swiss hospital to receive the birthday news. It was a daughter, called Yasmin Aga Khan, who had her mother's beautiful features, and would receive her father's doting attention.

The world labeled this little girl fortunate indeed, but life was to prove otherwise. The celebrated marriage of her parents crumbled when Yasmin was almost two years old. Rita, who had returned from Europe to the United States with her daughter, divorced Aly Khan in 1953.

Despite the distance that separated them, Yasmin spent nearly every summer with her father in Europe; they rode horseback, played tennis, and went boating together. "My father was wonderful, very loving and caring. He made everything beautiful and magical," she recalls.[1] But when Yasmin was ten years old, tragedy struck; Aly Khan was killed in an automobile accident while driving one of his race cars.

Yasmin relied on her strong emotional bond with her mother to cope with his death. And her memories of early childhood and her parents remain positive. "I was very fortunate growing up. I had the foundation of love. On both sides, the support was there."[2]

As she developed, it became clear that this princess had inherited a talent to perform. Unlike her mother, who had made a name for herself first as a dancer and then as an actress, Yasmin showed singing ability. Actually, her mother loved to sing, but her voice was not good enough for the Hollywood musicals in which she starred.

Yasmin, on the other hand, showed first-rate singing ability from the time she was fifteen and a student at the Buxton School, a private school in Massachusetts. After graduating from high school, she majored in music at Bennington College, studying music composition as well as training her lyric coloratura voice. When she was in her early twenties, Yasmin continued to work on her singing. At age twenty-six, she auditioned for a famous German conductor, who offered to give her nonstop training for two years on the understanding that Yasmin had the talent to become a world-class singer.

It was at that critical point in her life that Princess Yasmin Aga Khan confronted a heartache. For several years, her mother had seemed disturbed, sometimes acting irrationally and having violent mood swings. At first, her friends and family analyzed the behavior as stemming from Rita's personal troubles. Maybe she's disappointed in not being offered acting parts, they said; maybe she's angry about getting older, or, most probably, they guessed, she's drinking too much.

The symptoms became worse, however, and in 1978, after a two-year search for medical answers, Rita Hayworth was diagnosed as having Alzheimer's disease.

Alzheimer's is a fatal brain disorder that is difficult to recognize at first because the person with the disease seems merely confused and forgetful at times. "My mother was still trying to keep her career as a movie star, trying to memorize lines and all, but her brain wasn't functioning right. She was trying to hang on, to keep things together, but it was devastating, because she just couldn't cope," Yasmin remembers.[3]

To the general public, the disease was a type of mental instability, and there was little research being undertaken to study the illness. What was known is that Alzheimer's is a fatal disease that works slowly, gradually destroying the victim's ability to walk, speak, and even eat.

As her mother's condition got worse, everyone was still convinced that alcohol abuse was the problem. It wasn't until Rita had a severe breakdown that doctors finally recognized the disease.

It was at this time that Yasmin had to make her choice: pursue her musical ambitions by training in Europe or remain in New York in order to take care of her mother. Her decision was made without regret. "I went to help her. There was nothing else I wanted to do. That's when I got involved with Alzheimer's and when I gave up singing. I just stopped."[4]

Her uncommon maturity in this situation and in the years that followed was more than admirable. Singing had been her means of expression, yet she felt she couldn't ignore her foremost responsibility as a daughter. "I made the decision for another life," she says simply. She also credits her college education for opening her up to other possibilities. "I learned that there was more to life than music, that I could do more for people than just sing."[5]

Yasmin decided that her ailing mother should be cared for at home. She secured two apartments on the same floor of a building in New York City. Fortunately, Yasmin's elderly nanny still lived with her, and eighty-two-year-old Marie Walla helped Yasmin care for her mother, who became more and more bedridden in the early 1980s.

In a very direct way, Yasmin gave back to her mother the loving support she felt she had received as a child. Frustrated by the knowledge that her mother's battle with the disease could not be won, Yasmin made a decision to commit herself to the cause of finding a cure for Alzheimer's.

Toward that goal, she was ready to use her royal background, which had made her an aristocrat with socially prominent friends, people who would be able to donate money toward funding important medical research. She created events designed to raise this money, staging a Rita Hayworth Gala every year since 1985.

Yasmin also possessed glamour. With her auburn hair, brown eyes, and wide smile, she was nearly a mirror image of young Rita, whose face men adored in the 1940s. The "beautiful people," those with money to contribute to a good cause, were attracted by her stylishness as well as her title, and the press was eager to cover Yasmin's personal ordeal and her efforts on behalf of Alzheimer's.

Beyond the party-giving circuit, Yasmin became a well-informed spokesperson in educating people about Alzheimer's disease. She accompanied medical experts to Washington, D.C., to talk with senators and representatives about the importance of federal funding to combat the illness. She could take credit, too, for the result of this effort, if she weren't basically a modest, unassuming individual. In 1980, when she started her campaign, there was only $13 million for Alzheimer's research; seven years later, the Alzheimer's and Related Disorders Association raised $65 million in its annual drive.

In 1985, Princess Yasmin Aga Khan, then thirty-five, became attracted to Basil Embiricos, a Greek shipping heir. The two exchanged wedding vows in a Paris ceremony that was attended by 500 guests and hosted by Yasmin's half brother, His Highness the Aga Khan IV, who, in place of his father, Aly Khan, had been named the spiritual leader of the Muslim people. Yasmin's mother was not well enough to see the ceremony.

Within the year, Yasmin gave birth to a son, Andrew. The marriage did not work out, however, and Yasmin was left to raise the child by herself.

Recovering from her failed marriage, Yasmin talked about how she would help her young child cope with the unhappy situation. "I think you've got to be as honest as you can. You can't make up beautiful stories and paint everything rosy. Most important, though, if there was once love in a relationship, you've got to tell the children that there *was* love."[6]

Life is filled with bitter lessons, she feels. "To survive, Andrew has to know that the world is not the storybook world you see on Walt Disney and in fairy tales." Imagination and fantasy should be encouraged, she says, adding that her son should know, too, "the harder reality and how to deal with it. If you can find that equilibrium [a sense of balance] within yourself, you have a head start. Then he can go out into the world and fight the battles and have the self-esteem and the strength and the courage that he needs."[7]

Yasmin has drawn on this courage many times over. Her mother lost the struggle with Alzheimer's in 1987, yet her death only made Yasmin more resolved to continue her full-fledged fight against the disease.

Today, Yasmin is active in two organizations devoted to Alzheimer's research, serving as president and vice chairman for the groups. She also acts as the general chairman for the Rita Hayworth Galas, recruiting influential, wealthy friends to join her in supporting the charity.

The celebrity scene is not appealing to her in spite of her activism. "I'm more of an in-the-background kind of person," she says, acknowledging that she has to overcome her natural shyness to play the role of official hostess.[8]

Her royal lineage is apparent in the way she has decorated her home. It is Islamic in character, with antiques, Oriental rugs, family pictures, and Old World prints giving the rooms a lived-in richness. Explaining the traditional furnishings, the contemporary princess says, "I have a genuine appreciation for art and antiques, and I enjoy collecting things with a past or family history. They become part of me and create the only atmosphere in which I feel truly at home."[9]

Through the hardships, Yasmin has had a loyal band of close friends to provide support. But she insists that one can only rely on oneself to get through troubled times. In the fairy tales, a princess is taken care of, her wishes are granted, but it's Yasmin's hardened belief that independence is the best ready-position for life.

In her realistic view, her mother's ordeal "made me responsible as a mother," she says. The disease forced her to examine what was truly important. "I've always had to make all those crucial decisions myself. You learn to be self-reliant. In taking care of my own parent, I've had to make difficult choices. Responsibility doesn't frighten me anymore."[10]

In February 1989, Yasmin had reason to celebrate: She married one of her "close friends," real estate developer Christopher Jeffries. With little Andrew, she and her new husband plan to continue living in New York City.

A princess with a mission, she has become a soldier of sorts. Yasmin has the determination to reach her goal, and as an added gift from Allah (the Supreme Being of the Muslim faith), has the talent to make her royal background benefit others.

## H.R.H., PRINCESS
## DIANA OF WALES

When nineteen-year-old Lady Diana Frances Spencer said "I will" during a wedding ceremony broadcast to more than one billion people all over the world, she wasn't just making a marriage vow. In the moment it took to say those two words she not only went from maiden to matron, but from nobility to royalty. She also was saying "I will" to a very serious role as Princess of Wales and consort to Prince Charles. Unsaid but understood was that, instantly, she would also become the future queen of England. Either way you look at it, the rite of passage on that sunny day in July 1981, committed Diana to a life not only of great privilege but also of great responsibility.

There are lots of girls and women who would love to be in her shoes, even with the crushing responsibility. It's a pretty heady experience, being courted by a prince, falling in love with him, having that love returned, and becoming a princess. The mere idea of it is the basis for fairy tales in dozens of cultures. To become an instant celebrity, to become admired by millions of well-wishers, to know that you, by simple virtue of marrying the future king of England, are influencing world history—these are strong arguments in favor of accepting a royal proposal of marriage.

There is, of course, the massive wealth to consider: the royal palaces to call home, the glamorous jewelry, the closets full of designer clothes, the great staff of servants, the travel, the entrance into a charmed social circle. These are also pretty strong arguments in favor of saying "I will."

On the other hand, the flip side of all this glamour and excitement is the hard truth that being a modern-day English princess often has less to do with romance than duty and obligation. Being the Princess of Wales is a full-time job—a job from which there is no vacation, no chance to change your mind and try something else. It's a lifelong commitment, and, for Diana, there's no looking back.

There may be no looking back for Diana, but for the rest of the world there's plenty of looking *in*. The princess is one of the most photographed women in the world; the images of her beauty smile back at us from magazines, newspapers, television, and videos, in nearly every known language. From her perspective, it must seem as if every move she makes is covered by the press—every smile, yawn, frown, giggle, kiss, wave, crossing of the legs, or straightening of the hat or hem. Every action and comment is noted, studied, and criticized. She can't have a spat with her husband without it making the front page of the next morning's paper. If she wears the same dress twice on an official visit, she gets scolded by the press. If she tries to go anywhere incognito there's some sneaky photographer to snap at her with his camera. "Diana's life is a life in a royal fishbowl," sighed a friend. Life in that fishbowl means millions of people to please, millions of smiles to smile, millions of flashbulbs in her face . . . and rarely, if ever, any privacy.

Ultimately, too, it means a great deal of loneliness.

Despite these built-in frustrations, Diana, at twenty-seven, has risen beautifully to the occasion. She's earned the respect of one of her toughest critics, her mother-in-law, the queen, and she's arguably the most popular royal since Queen Victoria. In the years she's been in the public eye she's grown from a gangly, shy teenager into a regal young woman—elegant and charming, warm-hearted and enchanting.

Still, her new poise hasn't gone straight to her head. In many respects she's still the same Shy Di who captivated the world in 1981. She still giggles when she's nervous, blushes easily, and bites her nails—what she calls a "terrible" habit.

She's the first to admit that her strongest point isn't her intellect. She claims she's got "a brain the size of a pea,"[1] even though she's learned the fine—and difficult—art of making conversation.

She loves hats, trash novels, Kit Kat candy bars, rock and roll music, chewing gum, and dancing till dawn—not the typical pursuits of a princess. She can also shop until she drops, to the chagrin of her husband, who hates to spend money (even though he has plenty of it).

But lest she sound a bit immature, she does have her serious, accomplished side. She's almost singlehandedly brought the English royal family to its current high level of popularity—both in Britain and the rest of the world. She's a tireless fundraiser for charity. And she's a devoted mom to two cute, energetic young princes.

It's a life that even Diana couldn't have dreamed would turn out this way . . . and she *did* dream, as most English girls do, of marrying a prince. When news of her relationship with Prince Charles leaked, her old school chums gleefully pointed out that when most of them were teenagers they had crushes on cute actors and rock stars. Diana Spencer was different—*she* was half in love with Prince Charles.

As fate would have it, her dream would come true, but living happily ever after in real life is turning out to be a little different from the way it happens in fairy tales. How she got where she is is a story that rivals the best fairy tale.

The Honourable Diana Frances Spencer was born on July 1, 1961. She has two older sisters, Lady Sarah and Lady Jane, and a younger brother, Charles, Lord Althorp, who will become the ninth Earl of Althorp upon his father's death. Between her father, Edward John Spencer, the eighth Earl of Althorp, and her mother, Frances Roche, Diana's lineage actually has more royal blood than the House of Windsor, Prince Charles's family. She's related to

English, Scottish, Spanish, Dutch, and French kings; several U.S. Presidents, including George Washington; authors Noah Webster, who wrote the original Webster's Dictionary, and Louisa May Alcott; and even actors Humphrey Bogart and Lillian Gish. Ironically, too, she's related to her own husband— Prince Charles is her seventh cousin once removed!

Diana and her sisters and brother were raised in the Park House, a ten-bedroom mansion on the Royal Sandringham Estate, a stone's throw from where Diana's future husband spent vacations. It wasn't unusual for the Spencer children to see the queen or other royals riding in the park, and the queen would often stop and chat with them. Little did Queen Elizabeth know she was speaking with her future daughter-in-law! The Spencers were raised in a nursery wing by a strict nanny. Diana was a gorgeous baby, with a rosy complexion and silky white-blonde hair her two big sisters loved to brush and play with.

Park House was a wonderful house to grow up in. Besides the great garden and beautiful grounds, the house, filled with antiques and family portraits, was near the beach. Diana had a charmed early childhood. But when she was six, the bubble burst. The Spencer kids were told that their parents were undergoing a trial separation. They never reconciled; in 1969, they divorced.

It was unusual for the time, but custody of the four Spencer children went to their father. Their mother soon married her lover, Peter Shand Kydd, and left England, where she was a countess, to be a sheep farmer's wife. The Shand Kydds divided their time between two farms, one on an island off the coast of Scotland, the other in Australia. In mid-1988, to Diana's dismay, the Shand Kydds decided to divorce.

With her father a single parent, it was a logical choice to send Diana off to boarding school. She made the adjustment well even though it must have been difficult to leave home at such a young age. Actually, she blossomed at West Heath School. There she excelled at swimming and tennis, and in her last year she was made a prefect—a student monitor—and was given an award for service to the school.

Diana was popular, but academically she didn't do very well. In fact, the princess flunked every O-level exam—a kind of achievement test—in *every* subject.

What she may have lacked in academic skill she more than made up for in charm and personality. Still, formal education never suited her.

In 1978, when she was seventeen, she enrolled in a Swiss finishing school, but only stayed for six weeks. She returned to England and supported herself doing odd jobs—teaching classes for three-year-olds at a dance studio and, like the fictitious Cinderella, cleaning apartments. She finally found a job she adored, as an assistant kindergarten teacher and part-time nanny. (It was never hard to tell that Diana loved children. Little did she know then that one of her own children would be the future King of England.)

How do you get a prince to notice you, much less ask you out? For Lady Diana Spencer, it was a combination of luck, perseverance, and an unlikely pair of fairy godmothers—her maternal grandmother, Lady Ruth Fermoy, and Charles's grandmother, Queen Elizabeth, the Queen Mother.

Diana had nurtured a crush on Prince Charles ever since she was in boarding school. In her dormitory, Diana had a photo of Charles above her bed.

Imagine her surprise when her older sister, Lady Sarah, started dating Charles in 1977. He had been invited to a weekend pheasant-shooting party at Althorp. Charles and Diana were formally introduced then, but the setting was hardly ideal; they met in a muddy, just-ploughed field. Diana's reaction: the prince was "pretty amazing." Later, Charles was to say that he found Diana "amusing and attractive . . . bouncy and full of life."[2]

The romance between Sarah Spencer and Charles didn't last long, however. Charles and Di weren't to meet again until two years later. This time it was sister Jane who set the scene for the romance.

Lady Jane's husband, Robert Fellowes, was then assistant private secretary to the queen. He frequently traveled with her to help keep her royal affairs in order. In 1979, he accompanied her to Balmoral, a royal residence in Scotland, during the queen's annual vacation. Diana came along with the Felloweses to help take care of their new baby daughter. Prince Charles was at Balmoral, too. As the story goes, Lady Fermoy mentioned to the Queen Mother that Diana was keen on Prince

Charles, and the Queen Mother passed this little tidbit of information along to her grandson.

When the two met up again, the prince was delighted to hear that the girl he'd met on a shoot two years before had matured into a lovely young woman. At first, Charles treated her like the girl next door. She was great fun, always quick to laugh, and she didn't seem at all awed by royalty. Not really looking to get involved—he had just broken up with a girlfriend—Charles found himself charmed. Gradually the friendship turned to romance, helped, it is said, by the Queen Mother's gentle suggestion that he consider Diana as a suitable marital partner.

Ironically, marriage prospects for the prince were fairly limited. Despite his position he couldn't just marry any woman he wanted. His wife had to be the right religion—Church of England; she had to be of child-bearing age, since producing an heir to the throne would be her and his number one priority; she had to have led a pristine past, so no scandal could bring embarassment to the royal family. What Charles saw in Diana was a remarkably lovely young woman who perfectly fit the bill. The icing on the cake was that she was clearly crazy about him and proved able to handle herself well under all sorts of stressful circumstances.

After a five-month courtship, Prince Charles proposed on February 3, 1981. Instead of being entirely romantic, the Prince was also practical. He warned Diana from the start about what she was letting herself in for: the lack of privacy, the whole world watching her every move, the never-ending royal responsibilities and the limits they would put on her independence. He suggested she take some time to consider. "I wanted to give her a chance to think about it," he explained. "To think if it was all going to be too awful."[3] But Diana didn't need to be asked twice. She accepted.

For the few months between engagement and wedding, Diana was tutored in the fine points of protocol—to whom she should curtsey, how to refer to her husband (in private, Charles; in public, sir) and her mother-in-law (Ma'am), and so on. There were endless meetings with designers and decorators, the former to create her wedding gown and the latter to outfit her new home in Kensington Palace. Everywhere she went—out to buy jeans, make a telephone call, even to the bathroom—she was followed by a detective from Scotland Yard. As the wedding day approached, for security purposes, Diana was moved into a small apartment in Buckingham Palace where she was carefully chaperoned.

The wedding itself was a spectacular affair. Some called it the wedding of the century; others boasted it was the wedding of the *millenium*! More than one million well-wishers showed up, jammed along the route as her glass carriage made its way to St. Paul's Cathedral. The ceremony was conducted by the Archbishop of Canterbury, who continued the Cinderella imagery begun in the popular press. "Here is the stuff," he pronounced, "of which fairy tales are made."[4] After a honeymoon on the Mediterranean aboard the royal yacht *Britannia*, the couple set up house at Kensington Palace.

Now, as a member of the House of Windsor, Diana will become the queen of England when Charles succeeds his mother. She'll be following several strong-minded women who have held the title in the past hundred years, notably Queen Victoria, the strict ruler who governed England from the time she was eighteen until her death at age eighty-two, and the present Queen Elizabeth, who has worn the crown since 1952, taking power when she was only twenty-five.

Unlike the future queen, both Victoria and Elizabeth inherited the throne, and were, therefore, the rightful rulers of the country. Their husbands, known as "consorts," forever carry the title of prince, and are expected to play a supporting role to their wives. When Lady Diana Spencer became Princess of Wales, she also acquired several other titles—as well as an amazing amount of wealth. She's also Countess of Chester, Countess of Carrick, Duchess of Cornwall, and Duchess of Rothesay. She doesn't have to worry much about practical things like bills. The Duchy of Cornwall grosses about $3 million a year. The rest of Charles's fortune is estimated at $680 million.

Diana owns or has access to an astonishing collection of royal jewelry, including the magnificent tiara she wore at her wedding. Most of these gems have fascinating royal histories; all are priceless. And if her own jewels aren't right for an occasion, Diana has been known to borrow a piece or two from the queen.

Despite having a chauffeur at her disposal, Diana likes to drive herself around town. Her car of choice is a Ford Sierra. She is also allowed to use a $170,000 Bentley and a Jaguar. When she does drive herself, she's never really alone—her detective/bodyguard sits next to her, and others follow in another car. And when she drives, she likes to drive *fast*. Twice she's been pulled over for speeding. But she got off both times with a warning.

She also has four royal palaces to call home. It might seem strange that the royal couple and their two sons live in an apartment, but remember that the apartment (actually two put together) is a twenty-five-room triplex in Kensington Palace. The Palace was built in 1689 and faces a glorious park. Sharing the colossal building are Princess Margaret (Charles's aunt), Princess Michael of Kent (the Queen's cousin), and the Duke of Gloucester. The surroundings are glamorous and the price is right—it's free.

The apartment is as luxurious as you'd expect. There's a wine cellar, his-and-hers dressing rooms, a dining room table that seats sixteen, and marble bathrooms. It also has its share of whimsy. In one of the downstairs bathrooms there's a collection of cartoons of the prince and princess from all over the world.

When the royal couple feels like getting away for the weekend, they drive to Highgrove, their 200-year-old, thirty-room, Georgian-style country home. To Diana, it's her dream house, and she was delighted to have been in charge of a $500,000 renovation. Weekends at Highgrove are designed for rest and relaxation. The little princes have their ponies there. There's an outdoor pool. Charles likes to hunt on the grounds or play polo. There are private ponds stocked with fish and wonderful gardens to work in or simply enjoy.

If even Highgrove feels humdrum, there's also Craigowen in Scotland and a cottage called Tamarisk in the Scilly Isles near Cornwall. And the couple is always welcome at any other royal residence in the British Isles.

What's it really like to be the Princess of Wales? Says diplomatic Princess Di: "seventy percent slog [English slang for drudgery] and thirty percent fantastic."[5]

The fantastic part you might guess; the slog part is the price she has to pay for it. It's the realistic, not-very-fairy-tale-like side of being a princess: the duty. Never mind how boring it can all be, and never mind that part of the game is not to betray how tedious the endless rounds of official functions are.

There are ribbon-cutting ceremonies to attend, tours of industrial plants, power stations, army barracks, factories, and hospitals. Diana made headlines when she shook hands with an AIDS patient and didn't wear gloves. She helped demonstrate that casual contact with AIDS victims isn't dangerous. She's often asked to plant trees. There are long dinners with business people and foreign dignitaries, where she's expected to at least look interested, even if the discussion is frightfully boring. She has had to learn the difficult art of small talk, so she can make charming, informed chitchat on any number of topics, from world affairs to cultural events to sports. She's frequently expected to give speeches. She often writes these talks herself, but public speaking is still nerve-wracking for her. Before any tour or social event, she studies facts about the countries she visits, their people, culture, and history. She also memorizes details about her host's or guests' biographies. Often, she's on her feet for hours at a time, smiling even though her cheeks may get numb and her feet may hurt.

One of her biggest jobs is to promote England around the world. The prince and princess spend about five weeks a year on tour to help generate publicity for Britain and its products and services. In her first seven years of marriage, she's made official visits, called "walkabouts," to nineteen different countries—including Australia, Thailand, the United States, Canada, New Zealand, Fiji, Italy, and Japan. The excitement of travel is counterbalanced by enormous fatigue and homesickness. Despite having an entourage that includes a butler, Diana's lady-in-waiting and hairdresser, Charles's valet, their equerry (an officer of the British royal household), a private secretary, royal physician, assistant dresser (Diana usually changes clothes four times a day), several security officers, a baggage master, and the private secretary's secretary, the trips are exhausting. There are official meetings, meals, tours, and photo sessions to attend, and there's rarely a minute to herself. Diana holds up well throughout the walkabouts and rarely complains. Needless to say the tours are nearly always smashing successes.

Back home, her public appearances are more often than not tied in with charity events. At last count, she was patron or president of twenty-nine British charities, many of which reflect her love of children and dance or are personal causes in some way. She's active in cancer research, partly because her father has had lung cancer.

Diana takes her charity work very seriously. She doesn't limit her activities to the personal appearances she makes, which average four to five per week. She also writes letters, gives speeches, and helps with fundraising drives.

Why such commitment? She says, "I don't want to dive into something without being able to follow it up. Nothing would upset me more than just being a name on top of a piece of paper and not showing any interest at all."[6] She's even learned sign language to help her work on behalf of the British Deaf Association.

As for a career other than being a "career princess," there's virtually no chance that Diana would ever hold a paying job like her sister-in-law Sarah has. It simply isn't done; she hasn't the freedoms the Duchess of York enjoys. Instead of career, she looks at her work as being the power behind the throne, so to speak. "I feel my role is supporting my husband whenever I can," she says, "and always being behind him, encouraging him. And also, most important, being a mother and wife."[7]

It's no secret that Diana adores children. She longed for some of her own even before she met Charles. She's dropping hints that she'd like another child or two—preferably of the female sort. She so enjoys motherhood that she's commented that being a princess isn't her first priority, being a mother is. She shines in the limelight, but her favorite role is mum to William Arthur Philip Louis and Henry Charles Albert David.

Being a mother is so important to her that she's defied royal tradition several times. One way is by active participation in the day-to-day parenting chores that, in aristocratic families, usually are left exclusively to nannies and governesses. Instead of having a rather stiff, formal relationship with her sons, Diana plays with them constantly, feeds and bathes them, all in an attempt to raise them as "normal children." She has borne her share of criticism for her decision—from her mother-in-law on down. Some find her comment a bit naive—after all, how normal can it be to be a prince, to live in a palace, be saluted, and have two round-the-clock nannies, two detectives, and three footmen?

Still, like most mothers, Diana's strict about some things—mostly junk food (reserved for special occasions) and TV, even if she's a bit overindulgent in other areas (she really has to be pushed before she scolds or punishes them).

What's a typical day in the life of the Princess of Wales like? Her routine varies, depending on whether her day is jam-packed or low-key. She usually wakes up around 7:00 A.M. and starts her day with a cup of coffee and some pop music. Then she slips into sweats for the ten-minute drive to the pool at Buckingham Palace. Diana is an avid swimmer and tries to get in her twenty laps every day. By 8:00, she's back at Kensington Palace, where she eats breakfast with her husband.

If she has a public appearance to make that day, her hairdresser comes to the palace to do her hair. She puts on her own makeup—a ritual that takes about twenty minutes. If she's working, she's usually out the door by 10:00.

On the days when Diana is not working, she likes to play tennis at the Vanderbilt Racquet Club. And about once every two weeks, she meets a friend or two for lunch. For security reasons, tables are booked a day in advance, one table for Diana and her friends, another for her detective. Diana doesn't receive a royal discount, and since, as tradition dictates, she doesn't carry money, the tab is either picked up by her friend, or sent to her office.

After lunch, she likes to shop. She's also known to drop by a rehearsal of the London City Ballet, of which she is a patron.

Once back at home, she usually practices the piano. Diana's quite an accomplished player, and has mastered several intricate pieces of classical music. When she's not playing, she'll catch up on her correspondence until 4:00. Then it's teatime, that great English tradition. It gives her the chance to play with her boys and to socialize with her friends and their kids.

On those nights when she has no plans to go out (Charles and Diana socialize about four nights a week), she'll read the children their bedtime story. By the time they're asleep, it's about 9:00, when she and Charles can sit down for a dinner that's prepared by their chef. Diana chooses the week's menu every Monday. Her favorite foods are fish, pasta, and vegetables.

After dinner, Diana indulges herself with TV. She's partial to soaps, particularly "Dynasty" and "EastEnders" (an English series). Bedtime is usually 10:30, and she often retires with a book.

Charles and Diana love being homebodies, but in the early years of their marriage they rarely entertained at home. Lately, though, they've gotten a bit more into the party spirit and like to throw lavish, black-tie parties about twice a week. The guest list often reads like a who's who of the rich, noble, famous, and powerful.

When Charles is out of town or off on a royal duty of his own, Diana has the perfect chance to host a girl's night and invites five or six of her closest friends from her school days. Diana reportedly loves these nights, when she can forget she's a princess and can be carefree—at least for a little while. Even for princesses, the grass is sometimes greener on the other side.

## H.R.H., THE
## DUCHESS OF YORK

Officially, her title is Her Royal Highness, The Princess Andrew, Duchess of York. Her husband, Prince Andrew Albert Christian Edward, Queen Elizabeth II's second son, calls her "Biggles" (after a swashbuckling English pilot); the royal family refers to her as Sarah York. In public her friends are required by protocol to call her "Ma'am," but in private they get to call her Sarah.

To most people, however, she's simply Fergie, a name both she and Andrew detest. But that's what the press calls her, and that's what her many admirers call her, so the dreaded nickname remains.

Tall and witty, with a sunny disposition and a gorgeous mane of shiny red hair, the twenty-nine year-old duchess has made quite an impression as the newest member of the royal family. Her warm personality and sense of humor add spice to the ranks that have, on more than one occasion, been labeled stuffy. Not only is her style unique, but in the short time she's been a member of the Windsor clan she has blazed all sorts of new paths. She's the first female royal, for instance, to keep her job after marriage. She's the first to learn how to fly. She's the first to have her own house built, preferring a new one to an apartment in one of the many posh royal residences at her disposal.

She's also the first woman to tame Prince Andrew. Before they fell in love, he was known to be a bit of a devil-may-care playboy, rather arrogant and overbearing. But marriage and a baby—Beatrice Elizabeth Mary, nicknamed "Beetroot," born August 8, 1988—have changed all that. Andrew has matured and mellowed, and Sarah has evolved from a chatty, rebellious young woman into a more polished sophisticate. Popular with the royal family and the press, Sarah has also won the heart of most of the rest of the world.

The Sarah-Andrew love story actually begins with Diana, Princess of Wales. She played Cupid magnificently by strategically encouraging a romance between her brother-in-law and one of her dearest friends.

The two women had become close the year before Diana got married. Sarah's flat-mate (a flat is what the English call an apartment) was the cousin of Diana's lady-in-waiting, and the four of them got along very well. Although Sarah was two years older than Lady Diana, they found they had much in common. Both were "Sloane Rangers"—the London equivalent of preppies. Both had parents who divorced when their daughters were young. Both were raised by their fathers. They also shared a fondness for shopping and gossiping and partying til the wee hours. After Diana's wedding, Sarah would come to Kensington Palace to lunch with her at least once a week, and they talked every day on the phone. Sarah, more worldly than her shy, less experienced friend, often gave good advice on how to handle the pressures of life in the royal spotlight. For her part, Diana was a sympathetic listener when Sarah relayed the latest complications in her love life.

Prince Charles may have been the first and only love of Diana's life, but by the time Sarah became involved with Andrew she had had two long-term relationships. The first was with Kim Smith-Bingham, a dashing English stockbroker who ran a ski equipment business in Verbier, a ski resort in the Swiss Alps, where Sarah often went on holiday. The second boyfriend was Paddy McNally, a widower twenty years her senior. Charming and wealthy, a journalist, race-car driver and manager, he introduced Sarah to life in the fast lane. McNally, who had two teenage sons, cared deeply for Sarah but wasn't as keen on marriage as she was. When the two of them decided to call it quits, Diana rushed to the rescue. She made sure Sarah was invited to join the royal party during Ascot Week, the annual horse races that are a favorite social event of the Windsors.

This wasn't the first time Sarah and Andrew had met. In fact, they'd known each other casually for most of their lives. Sarah knew Andrew's brother Prince Charles through her father, Major Ronald Ferguson, a former cavalry officer and Prince Charles's polo manager. As children, she and Andrew, who's five months younger than she is, often played together. As adults, they were nodding acquaintances, nothing more. But at Ascot, matchmaker Diana made sure they rode together in an open-carriage and sat next to each other at a formal luncheon.

It was at this elegant lunch that they noticed—really noticed—each other. Later, Sarah would laughingly admit that it was a chocolate profiterole that brought them together. Apparently Andrew tried to tease her into eating the rich dessert (pastry and ice cream covered in chocolate) when she really didn't want to. "I was meant to be on a diet,"[1] she explained merrily. In a bit of a teasing mood herself, Sarah responded to his taunts by throwing one of the gooey things at him.

Wasn't the Prince offended by her nerve? Hardly. A bit of a prankster himself (he once sprayed photographers with a paint gun), Andrew thought her high jinks hilarious and asked her out.

It wasn't long before romance bloomed. Andrew turned out to be thoughtful, romantic—and smitten. He sent dozens of bouquets of long-stemmed red roses and wrote love letters discreetly signed "A." Andrew and Sarah did a good job of keeping their relationship a secret, but after they were seen holding hands at Sandringham Palace a few months later, the word spread like wildfire. Reporters and photographers hounded Sarah mercilessly, the way they had Diana six years before. Sarah benefitted by her friend's experience and quickly became adept at ducking the press. Her flat-mate would act as a decoy, wearing sunglasses and driving off in Sarah's car. The press still followed the real Sarah everywhere, even onto the black (expert) ski trails in the Alps! Sarah was good-natured about the deluge and has remained so to this day.

During the courtship, Sarah's friends couldn't help but notice how happy she'd become. The romance with Andrew restored the self-confidence that had been battered during her up-and-down affair with Paddy McNally. Happy too was Andrew's mum, the queen, who had made little secret of how she felt about Andrew's previous girlfriends. Elizabeth was reportedly overjoyed at the idea of Sarah as a daughter-in-law. Also rooting for a royal marriage were Diana, of course, and Andrew's sister, Princess Anne, and brothers, Charles and Edward, all of whom found Sarah delightful and a wonderful influence on the prince.

Sarah got an idea of her future husband's intentions when he gave her a pair of gold heart-shaped earrings for Christmas in 1985. According to royal-watchers, a gift of jewelry from a royal is a between-the-lines hint that things are getting pretty serious. Still, she was surprised when in February 1986, Andrew got down on both knees and proposed.

At first, Sarah thought he was joking. She said yes anyway, telling him, "When you wake up tomorrow morning, you can tell me it's all a huge joke."[2]

Andrew wasn't joking. They were married on July 23, 1986, in front of 1,500 guests.

Can a leopard ever change its spots? In Andrew's case, apparently so. He hardly seems to miss his bachelor days, declaring marriage to Sarah to be "the best decision in my life . . ."[3] [she] is vivacious, cheerful, outgoing, vibrant. She sparkles, radiating warmth and a sense of fun . . . I think married life is wonderful."[4]

Sarah does too, even though marriage to a prince is a much bigger challenge than marrying the boy next door. However, she has adjusted beautifully to the demands of royal family life, sudden fame, official duties, and the often conflicting demands of work, marriage, and motherhood.

Sarah Margaret Ferguson was born in Sunninghill, near Ascot, just outside of London. Her parents were well connected and well off. Though not technically members of the aristocracy, they did qualify as landed gentry. When Sarah was seven her father inherited Dummer Down House, a stately home set among 800 wooded acres (324 ha) in the Hampshire countryside.

Sarah grew up with seaside picnics and vacations in Cornwall. It was a happy time. She was outgoing, funny, and above all, athletic. She loved tennis and swimming but riding best of all. Her mother, an accomplished horsewoman, encouraged her daughters to follow in her footsteps. As a result, both girls could ride almost as soon as they could walk. Sarah won lots of prizes at pony-club contests. The family made it a practice to go to horse shows whenever possible, and there the Ferguson girls would play with Andrew and his younger brother Edward.

But Sarah was soon to know the heartbreak of divorce. When she was thirteen, her parents separated. Sarah's mother had fallen in love with an Argentinian polo player, Hector Barrantes. She and Major Ferguson were divorced in 1973. Shortly after the final decree, Susan Ferguson married Mr. Barrantes and moved with him to his ranch just outside of Buenos Aires. "It was a bit of a fright, to put it mildly,"[5] said Ronald Ferguson, referring to his ex-wife's departure for South America. "It meant that at a vulnerable age [the girls] didn't have Mother, so Father took over and did his best."

Her father later remarried. Sarah's stepmother is another Susan, Susan Deptford. According to all reports, both Ferguson daughters gave her a warm-hearted welcome into the family. "She [Sarah] was very close to her real mother, but she went out of her way to make me feel welcome,"[6] said the new Susan Ferguson. Susan Deptford Ferguson has three children, Sarah's two step-sisters and step-brother. Even with a considerable age gap, Sarah is close to all of her younger siblings.

Sarah and Jane had been at boarding school when news of the split came. They weren't totally surprised—by that time, her parents were frequently apart, separated by unsynchronized travel schedules and differing interests. But friends claim the divorce left deep scars. Some have even suggested that Sarah's often over-exuberant high spirits was her way to deal with the sadness, fear, and insecurity she felt when her world suddenly went upside-down, and her mother moved 6,000 miles (9,660 km) away. Says Jane: "The breakup affected us both. We are still close to our mother though we never saw as much of her as we did of Dad following the divorce."[7]

Sarah did well enough, not outstandingly, in school. Friends and former teachers remember her for her big smile and her fondness for pranks and practical jokes such as slipping frog's eggs into an unsuspecting girl's pocket and food fights.

She never seriously considered going to college. Instead, she went to secretarial school. This is a choice that might seem surprising for someone of her background and intelligence, but it's actually a common career path for young women of her class. So, at seventeen, she enrolled in the Queen's Secretarial College, where fellow pupils were debutantes and diplomats' daughters.

At school, Sarah went through the motions, preferring London's sensational social scene to practicing typing and shorthand. She shared a flat with cousins and tooled around town in the blue Volkswagen her father gave her.

Her first job was with a public relations firm owned by a friend of her father, Neil Durden-Smith. According to her boss, Sarah did extremely well there. She quickly learned how to handle difficult clients with tact, charm, and diplomacy—skills that would later give her an advantage in dealing with the demands of royal duty. "If I had a knotty problem or a difficult client, I would always bring Sarah in,"[8] says Durden-Smith. "She was able to get on with all sorts of people."

Shortly after she turned twenty-one, Sarah got a new job as an assistant in an art gallery. Again, she impressed her boss with her ease with people. "She was a super saleswoman with that knack of remembering clients and their tastes,"[9] recalled the art dealer, William Drummond. But the job didn't last long. When the lease ran out the gallery closed and Sarah was ready to try something different. Her then boyfriend, Paddy McNally, introduced her to an old race-car chum, Richard Burton (no relation to the actor). Burton, who lived in Geneva, Switzerland, had founded a successful publishing house, the kind that prints large, expensive books on art and architecture. He hired Sarah to be his London agent.

The job suited Sarah, and Sarah suited her position well, too. She grew to love editorial work so much that she announced she would be keeping her job even after joining the royal ranks. Some members of her family-to-be raised their royal eyebrows at her intentions, but Sarah was firm. She kept her job and was able to press her luck further when she announced that after the birth of her daughter she would continue to work—not full time, but on a freelance basis.

As an acquisitions editor, she works with writers, photographers, designers, copy editors, proofreaders, lawyers, printers, and literary agents, all of whom share in the collaborative process of producing a book. While still a full-time employee (she resigned at the end of 1987), she also directed regular editorial meetings. For security reasons, these were held at Buckingham Palace, which must have been quite an experience for even the most sophisticated writer.

The Duchess married into one of the world's wealthiest dynasties, so it's not the salary—rumored to be as high as $45,000 a year—that motivated her to continue working. It's simply that she finds her career very satisfying.

It also helps keep her challenged. Since Andrew is a career naval officer and will be until he's fifty-five, a job is an excellent way for Sarah to keep busy while he's at sea or stationed on base for long periods of time.

"The busier you are the more you get done," she has declared. "For me, [work] is a tonic. It keeps me in touch with the world around me."[10] She also seems to thrive under the intense pressure of deadlines. "It takes about twenty-five hours a day," she said, referring to her book projects, "but I just make sure there is time." Her secretary, she admitted, called her a "workaholic," which may, considering the evidence, be true. According to a former colleague, Sarah phoned one of her authors during her honeymoon to make sure his book was progressing smoothly!

Adding to an already hectic schedule are her royal duties, which include attending charity galas, opening special exhibitions, touring schools, hospitals, and factories, and making the occasional "walkabout", or royal tour, with her husband.

Sarah receives approximately ten written requests per week to help with fundraising efforts for various charities. So far, she's patron or president of eight organizations, whose interests range from countering drug abuse to promoting animal rights. In 1987 alone, she made a staggering 208 appearances. She also spearheaded "Search '88," a year-long series of events to raise money for cancer research.

Another favorite cause of Sarah's is the Tate Gallery Foundation, the organization that raises money to buy new works of art for the Tate Gallery, the world-renowned museum in London. It was this cause that brought Sarah to Greenwich, Connecticut, in the summer of 1987. There, an exclusive polo match and black-tie ball raised $500,000—mostly from people eager to pay $1,000 each for the privilege of dancing and sipping champagne near the duchess.

No matter how busy she is, however, she always tries to build in time for her new great passion, a hobby that requires great skill and daring. Lots of English princesses have been noted for their courage and love of adventure. After all, you can't be a championship horse jumper like Princess Anne *and* be a shrinking violet. But Sarah really made waves by fulfilling a promise she made to her husband early in their marriage . . . that she would learn to fly.

Flying lessons were a wedding gift. Sarah had casually mentioned that she wanted to learn more about it so she could discuss Prince Andrew's job intelligently with him.[11] Prince Andrew is a helicopter-pilot trainer and weapons specialist. As a pilot, she explains, "I can take an interest in my husband's career and know what he is talking about when he comes home at the end of the day."

Sarah took to flying like a natural. After only twenty-two days of training, she made her first solo flight. Air traffic controllers at the airfield where she made her first flight fondly dubbed her "Chatterbox One." She earned her wings in May 1987. Later that year, on a visit to an aerobatic flying team, she showed off a bit, executing barrel rolls and loop-the-loops to the enormous delight of the spectators. She won even more respect from her pilot peers when she earned her helicopter pilot license the following December. True to form, when she was pregnant with Beatrice, she announced she was planning to learn how to fly fighter jets—after the baby was born, of course.

What's a typical day in the life of the Duchess of York like? An early riser, Sarah's up and about at 6:30 A.M., when a maid brings a cup of tea. A typical breakfast is toast, yogurt, and fruit, which she eats while reading the London daily newspapers. After she's dressed, she usually heads to her office to do a little work or to catch up on her correspondence. Lunches aren't necessarily "power" lunches; she's more likely to dine in a restaurant with friends (and her bodyguard) than with other publishing types.

She also tries to fit in a daily fitness routine, not just to reduce stress but to help keep her weight down. The camera isn't always flattering to Sarah's curvy figure. She has a notorious sweet tooth, and she exercises diligently to keep in shape, but she hasn't always been successful at staying trim. The tabloid press has lately been a little cruel, calling her "Duchess Dumpy."

She helped her fitness cause by quitting smoking. She also keeps the champagne to an occasional glass and tries to watch what she eats. Soon after her engagement, she trimmed twenty-eight pounds by cutting out sweets and sticking to a low-fat diet that stressed chicken, fish, vegetables, and citrus fruits. After Beatrice was born, the weight she gained during her pregnancy wasn't so easy to take off. At five feet, seven inches (172 cm), she now weighs approximately 154 pounds (70 kg), about 15 or 20 pounds above her ideal weight.

Besides riding, swimming, and skiing, Sarah also works out at Body's Gym on Kings Road, a favorite of rocks stars and actors. She usually follows a program of aerobics and workouts on an exercise bike, and makes an occasional appearance on the Nautilus machines.

Prince Andrew's job keeps him on a naval base most weekdays, and he is at sea for up to eighteen weeks at a time. Sarah's evenings are rather quiet, unless she has a formal event to attend. Sometimes friends will come over for a dinner at Buckingham Palace. The meal is usually prepared by the queen's chef. Although Sarah has taken cooking classes, she claims she's something of a disaster in the kitchen.

Weekends serve as mini-reunions for Sarah and Andrew, who after three years of marriage still act like honeymooners. The Yorks often spend their time together in the country, either at the homes of relatives or at Castlewood House, a seven-bedroom mansion in Surrey that they rent from King Hussein of Jordan.

The couple is eagerly awaiting the completion of the house they can call their own, a $9 million mock-Tudor mansion, complete with a helicopter landing pad, stables and tack room, tennis courts, pool, and servant's quarters. There's also a nursery suite and the latest in high-tech security. The house is a wedding gift from Queen Elizabeth, and it's built near both the naval base (to make the commute easier) and Windsor Castle, where the queen likes to spend weekends.

The queen has taken especially kindly to Sarah, (the queen's relationship with her daughter-in-law Diana is more reserved and formal.) Sarah and Elizabeth often go riding in the mornings, enjoy long walks at the various royal palaces, and frequently have lunch together. Sarah has also won father-in-law Prince Philip's respect by learning the difficult sport of open-carriage racing, his personal favorite.

It's hard enough to win over the royal family, but Sarah Ferguson's managed to accomplish it quite handily. It's harder still to develop a worldwide following, but she's succeeded at becoming a media favorite with equal ability. It's clear that Sarah—also known as Fergie, Biggles, Princess, Duchess, and Chatterbox One—in her short stint as a Windsor, has been an entirely smashing success.

*Prince Rainier and Princess Grace of Monaco
with baby Princess Caroline in
one of her first official photographs*

*Caroline, nearly three years old, with her mother,*
*the former movie star, Grace Kelly*

*Princess Grace with baby*
*Stephanie in 1965*

*Monaco's Royal family in 1967.*
*Prince Rainier and Princess Grace with*
*Caroline (standing left), Albert (at right), and*
*Stephanie (center, in Princess Grace's arms).*

Left to right: *Princess Caroline
with her father, little Stephanie, Albert,
and her mother (wearing hat), at the
Monaco Dog Show in May 1969.*

*Ten-year-old Princess Stephanie*
*celebrating Monaco's centennial in 1975*

*In 1979, Princess Caroline led
a parade of hundreds of kids during
Children's Year in Monaco.*

*Princess Caroline at her
mother's funeral in September 1982*

*Princesses Caroline and Stephanie (left to right, both holding bouquets) accompany Prince Albert (behind Stephanie) and Prince Rainier (far right) to a Monaco gala in 1983.*

*Princess Caroline's husband, Stefano Casiraghi,*
*holds their daughter, Charlotte, as Caroline, holding*
*baby Pierre, listens attentively to her daughter.*
*The couple's first son, Andrea, is at right.*

*Princess Stephanie performs at a music*
*festival in Cannes, France, in 1987.*

*Princess Stephanie at Monaco's*
*annual Red Cross Ball*

*Princess Caroline in 1988*

*Princess Elizabeth of Toro (Uganda),*
*with her father, King George, in 1962*

*Twenty-year-old Princess Elizabeth at*
*Cambridge University in England*

*Princess Elizabeth as a fashion
model in London, 1968*

*In 1974, Princess Elizabeth became Uganda's
first female government minister.*

*The Crown Prince Harald of Norway and the
Crown Princess Sonja with Princess Martha Louise
at the baby's christening in 1971*

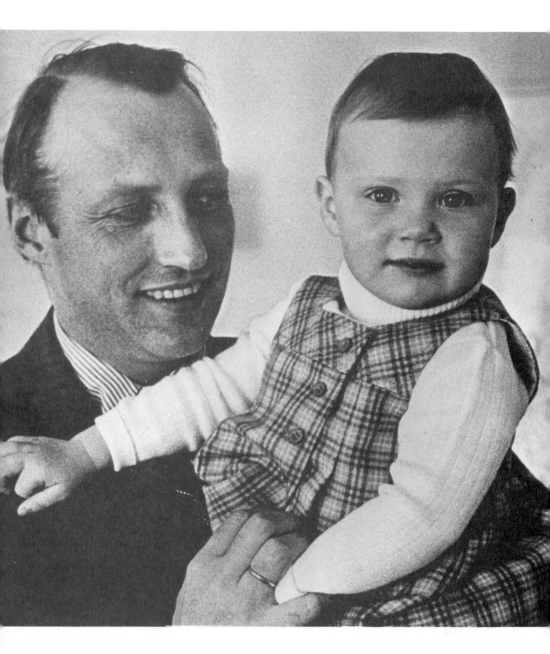

*Little Martha Louise with her father*

*Princess Martha Louise discusses the day's events with her schoolmates in Oslo.*

*Riding is Martha Louise's main interest. She has spent several summer holidays at British riding schools.*

*Princess Martha Louise (bottom right),*
*with her mom, dad, and brother,*
*Prince Haakon Magnus, in the summer of 1988*

*Princess Yasmin Aga Khan with her father,*
*Prince Aly Khan, in 1955*

*Twenty-year-old Princess Yasmin at London's*
*Heathrow Airport on a visit to her brother in England*

*Yasmin attending a New York Broadway premiere with
her mother, actress Rita Hayworth, in 1979*

*Princess Yasmin, at the Third Annual Rita Hayworth Gala to benefit Alzheimer's research, in 1986*

*Yasmin Aga Khan and Christopher Jeffries were married in New York in February 1989.*

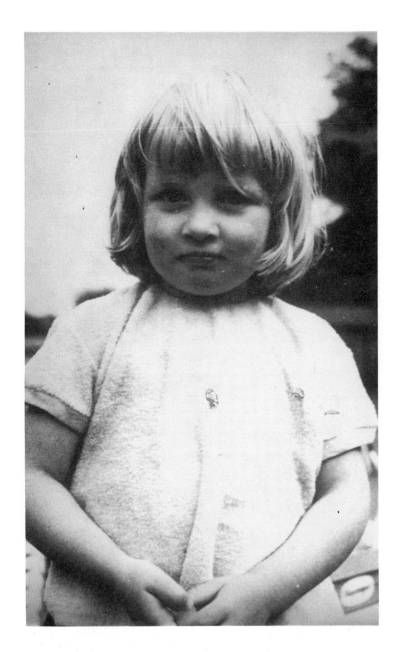

*Princess Diana of Wales at age three*

*Diana on vacation in summer 1970*

*Prince Charles poses with his then-fiancée,*
*Lady Diana Spencer, and his mother,*
*Queen Elizabeth, for the first time*
*at Buckingham Palace in March 1981.*

*On an official visit to the U.S. in 1985,
Princess Di visits a Virginia drug rehabilitation center
with then First Lady Nancy Reagan.*

*The prince and princess of Wales spend some
time with their son, little Prince William,
during an official visit to New Zealand in 1983.*

*Princess Diana has hold of her sons Prince William (right), and Prince Harry (left), in Scotland in 1986.*

*Sarah Ferguson at eighteen months*

*Sarah, now H.R.H., The Duchess of York,*
*with her teddy bear at age six*

*Sarah in July 1976, at her sister's wedding*

*Prince Andrew and Sarah Ferguson's wedding in 1986 was the "royal" event of the year.*

Sarah's flying lessons were a wedding gift from
Prince Andrew. After less than a year, "Fergie"
earned her wings and the respect of many British.

*The proud Duchess of York leaves
Portland Hospital in London with her new
baby daughter, Beatrice, in August 1988.*

*The Spanish Royal family in 1969.*
*Then-Princess Sofía—Prince Juan Carlos*
*was not crowned King until 1975—*
*holding Prince Felipe, poses with*
*Princess Elena, looking straight ahead,*
*and Princess Cristina, looking*
*up at her father, now the King of Spain.*

*Queen Sofía with (l. to. r.) Felipe, 8, Elena, 12, and Cristina, 10, at Heathrow Airport in London, in 1976*

*Princess Cristina, King Juan Carlos I,*
*Queen Sofia, Prince Felipe, and Princess Elena pose*
*for a recent family portrait in Madrid.*

*Princess Cristina with her mother in 1987*

*Princess Gloria von Thurn und Taxis in 1987*

*Sporting an eye-catching hairstyle,
Princess Gloria attends a ball honoring
Germany's contribution to opera, with
her husband, Johannes von Thurn und Taxis.*

*Princess Gloria photographed by world-famous*
*fashion photographer Helmut Newton*

*A young Catherine Oxenberg with her mother,*
*Princess Elizabeth of Yugoslavia, and Richard Burton,*
*at the actor's home in Hampstead, England*

*Catherine Oxenberg attending a 1984*
*Los Angeles movie screening*

*Catherine Oxenberg, left, receives a visit from
her mother on the set of "Dynasty."*

## PRINCESS ELENA
## AND PRINCESS CRISTINA
## OF SPAIN

When King Juan Carlos I was crowned as the new ruler of Spain in 1975, his two daughters, Elena and Cristina, then eleven and ten years old, were there to witness the event. Although they had been princesses since birth, the meaning of this title changed as their father accepted the lifelong pledge to govern the country.

Together with their younger brother, Felipe, the children became symbols of a new, hopeful spirit of Spain, a country that was emerging from many years of being controlled by a dictator. Although Spain voted to restore its monarchy in 1947, for years before and years afterward the decisions of government were made by a military dictator, General Francisco Franco. And it was only after he died, in 1975, that Juan Carlos and the royal family could voice their true hopes and beliefs for Spain.

Since then, Spain has become more of a democratic society under his command; the king is a royal who actively governs and has been able to keep the country stable. Together with Queen Sofia, he has created a stable family life, unlike the ones that they had when they were growing up.

In title, the king's daughters are H.R.H. Infanta Elena and H.R.H. Infanta Cristina, the *infanta* indicating "royal child." Both have learned from their parents that being of royal blood means much more than enjoying the riches and fame of privilege; it means serving the citizens of Spain in a responsible manner.

Now that the young girls have grown, the princesses have public duties as representatives of the Crown. But they are also building personal lives for themselves, working and studying for their careers outside the palace gates. Like their father, Elena and Cristina are down-to-earth Spaniards. They take their roles as members of royalty very seriously, but they haven't been spoiled by their position. They gladly participate in ceremonies, pageants, and special events that demand their presence, yet they enjoy the freedom of their own lives. Elena is a teacher, and Cristina is a student. Like most Spaniards, they enjoy the richness of life in a land that's known for its sunny skies, balmy seashore, and extremely friendly people.

Some palace-watchers compare Elena, the eldest child of King Juan Carlos and Queen Sofia, to her father. She's serious and shy, but she also has a competitive streak that makes her want to excel in sports. She is second in line for the throne, so that, after her brother, she is the rightful heir to inherit the power. To some extent this understudy position affects her life.

Elena was born on November 20, 1963, in a Madrid hospital. Her mother, Queen Sofia, was happy to have her sister and her parents, Queen Frederika and King Paul of Greece, present for the event. Three days later, Elena Maria Isabel Dominica de Silos was baptised at the royal family's home, the Zarzuela Palace.

Elena attended elementary and high school in Madrid. As a little girl, she had long blonde hair, and she and her sister would often be dressed alike, Cristina looking like a miniature of her. Now, Elena's hair is light brown; she's a little taller than her mother and much different in personality from Cristina.

Elena attended the Escuela University in Madrid. Since graduating in 1986, she has worked as an English teacher at the elementary school where she was once a student, Santa Maria del Camino. In addition to Spanish, she is fluent in English and knows German and French.

In her spare time, Elena loves to go to the ballet. Like her father, who is very athletic, she is a great sports lover, and shares his passion for sailing. During the winter, Elena joins the family on ski trips to the Pyrenees.

Being a royal gives Elena an unusual chance to travel. She's been to Japan as cultural ambassador for her country, and, as the Spanish royal family is very friendly with the British royals, there have been frequent trips to England. In July 1986, Elena attended the wedding of Prince Andrew and Sarah Ferguson. She also socializes with Prince Charles and Princess Diana, who take an annual summer holiday with the Spanish royal family at the seashore.

Elena has one travel restriction that doesn't apply to her sister. Because she is second in line for the throne, she is forbidden to live outside of Spain until her brother marries and has a child. The rule was bent somewhat to permit Elena to take university courses that would further her education. In 1987, she studied language and literature in Paris for a few months, and in 1988 completed a special education course at Exeter College in England.

Home for the Borbóns (the royal family's dynasty name) is a beautiful estate outside Madrid, Spain's capital city. When the king and queen were married in 1962, they were given this estate, the Zarzuela Palace, and have lived there since, despite the fact that they could live in the more opulent Royal Palace, with its 3,000 rooms, if they chose.

Zarzuela encompasses an elegant main house, once a hunting lodge, that is furnished with brightly colored furniture and accessories. It's a family home, decorated more with pictures of the parents and children than with delicate and expensive objects of art.

For the children, the palace was a playtime paradise because it sits in the middle of an enormous park, populated by all sorts of wildlife. Here, deer, rams, and even wild boar could roam the forests, and the three children could explore with their dogs.

By staying at Zarzuela when he became the country's leader, the king wanted to show his people that he was not interested in the regal trappings and that his leadership would encourage the country to become more democratic. The royal pomp and circumstance didn't figure into his objective. The royals are happy with their home near the forests a few miles removed from the hectic streets of Madrid.

The government's requirement that Elena stay in Spain has made her life more difficult. She had two romances that were stunted because of this responsibility she must carry. Duke Eberhard of Wurtemburg and Prince Kyril of Bulgaria were suitors, but marrying either would have been impossible, since this would have meant leaving Spain. On the other hand, neither Elena nor Cristina have to get approval for their marriages—unlike Prince Felipe, who must seek the consent of his parents and their advisors since his wife will one day be the queen of Spain.

Although these rules seem overly stern and strict, there is reason to protect the royal lineage, in King Juan Carlos's point of view. In contrast to his counterparts—the kings and queens of other European countries—Juan Carlos plays a much more important part in governing his country. He is not just a figurehead; as chief of the armed forces and the national leader capable of setting agendas for change, he wields real power. He has been a unifying symbol for Spain.

From the age of ten, Juan Carlos knew he would someday be king, but he could not know what the role would mean. Spain was controlled for thirty-nine years by General Franco, who had taken away many of the people's freedoms. Although Franco named Juan Carlos to be his successor, Franco probably never thought that this energetic, thoughtful man would actually take control of the country away from the military. What King Juan Carlos I did was to turn to the citizens. He called for elections immediately and won their support, and in 1981, he fought off an attempt by old Franco supporters to take his power away.

The king has become a very strong and respected leader. His six-foot, three-inch (192 cm) height, his serious nature, and his sense of formality make him the model of royalty. He was also wise enough to choose a wife with a winning, warm personality.

Sofia was "adopted" by the Spanish people. Born a Greek royal princess, Sofia met Juan Carlos for the first time when they were both sixteen years old. Over the years they were paired up at various events, and the two fell in love, much to the satisfaction of the Greeks and the Spaniards. Sofia stepped into her role as Juan Carlos's wife with little difficulty, although she did have to convert from being a Greek Orthodox to a Catholic, following the Spanish demands on royalty. Catholicism is the country's official religion.

Sofia, like Juan Carlos, had a lonely boarding-school upbringing, and possibly for this reason, the royal couple sought to make family life relaxed and happy for their children. Until the princesses could drive themselves, Queen Sofia shuttled them back and forth to their local schools, and she took an active role in supervising their hobbies, from leading them around the palace grounds on their ponies to encouraging them in piano practice. King Juan Carlos, an enthusiastic sportsman, included the children in his sailing afternoons, and boating remains an important part of the family's social schedule.

Elena may take her cues from her father's character, but Princess Cristina is closer to the outgoing Queen Sofia, despite the fact that having a second daughter—when a male heir was necessary for succession—was initially disappointing to Sofia. It is written that the queen burst into tears when she heard that the baby was a girl; she had been hoping for a son. As it happened, Felipe was born two and a half years later.

The Queen's first reaction must amuse her now, because Cristina (who was baptised Cristina Frederica Victoria Antonia de la Santisima Trinidad) has become a very popular member of the royal family, and the daughter who is especially close to her mother.

Outgoing, with a real spirit of fun and adventure, Cristina enjoys the opportunities to meet people in the course of her royal rounds. She has accompanied her parents on state visits to Thailand

and Nepal, and, with her sister, has been active in cultural and historical societies.

She was born on June 13, 1965, and attended the same elementary and high schools as her sister, who's only a year and a half older. When she turned eighteen in 1983, Cristina began making official appearances on behalf of her parents and acting as a hostess at parties and charity events.

That same year, she moved to London to study French and Greek, staying with her uncle and aunt. (Her uncle, King Constantine of Greece, lives in exile in England because the government of Greece no longer accepts him as the monarch.)

In 1984, Cristina returned to Spain and enrolled at the University of Madrid, taking courses in political science and anthropology, driving herself to and from campus every day. She received her degree in the spring of 1988. In addition to her native tongue, Cristina, like Elena, speaks English, Greek, and French quite well. When the little girls were growing up, their mother said, the children would speak Greek to each other when sharing secrets.

As hobbies, Princess Cristina enjoys playing the piano, having inherited musical talent from her mother, who's also an accomplished pianist. She and the queen traveled to New York City several years ago to attend an operatic recital featuring Spanish performers. Cristina is also a stamp collector, an avid reader (biographies are her favorite), and a good skier and squash player.

But her first love is sailing. For the past fifteen years, vacations for the Borbón family have centered around Majorca, where the royals relax in their summer home, the Palace of Marivent. They pilot their yacht, called *Fortune,* at the command of the king, who was a member of the Spanish Olympic sailing team in 1972. Cristina, her father, and her brother particularly enjoy these hours spent on the sea. She was a member of the 1988 Olympic team, competing for Spain in the yachting competition. She also carried the Spanish flag in the opening day ceremonies—undoubtedly the only princess on the field in Seoul, Korea.

Tall with blondish hair, Cristina is considered a very eligible princess in European social circles. With no rules imposed on whom she can marry or where she can live, she was serious at one point about Prince Luitpold of Bavaria, a champion race car driver who is a distant relative.

Until the right Prince Charmings present themselves, the young women of Zarzuela Palace are likely to stay in the royal nest where they can pursue their own personal goals and maintain their close family connection. The Spanish, meanwhile, applaud members of the royal family for their willingness to remain close to the people.

## PRINCESS GLORIA
## VON THURN UND TAXIS

Imagine being twenty years old, marrying a fabulously wealthy prince, and gaining in the bargain seventy-five personal servants, dazzling family jewels, six castles (including a 500-room palace), and a social calendar filled with elegant parties. Imagine, too, being this same princess and wanting to play the electric guitar, ride your motor bike, forget the makeup, and wear punk hairdos.

That sums up Gloria von Thurn und Taxis. Being a contemporary princess with a definite sense of style is what her life is all about.

Her nickname is Gloria von TNT—an indicator of a dynamite personality. She and her husband, Prince Johannes von Thurn und Taxis, rule no country (their title shows they are German aristocrats of long standing), but the two have set a different standard for royalty with their lavish life and her fun-loving approach to being privileged.

Princess Gloria, who married into incredible wealth, has exploded onto the royal scene, with the stiff and stuffy members of European society left wondering who this young woman in the weird clothes and with the broad smile really is. And how could she enjoy being with rock stars as much as sipping tea with elite socialites? But it's clear that Princess Gloria has the position and the wealth to party with whomever she pleases.

Her husband is the largest landowner in West Germany, having inherited his land and vast collections of antiques, rare books, gems, china, and stamps—not to mention mansions—from his German ancestors who date back to Franz the Rich, born in 1459. Because of their great wealth, the hereditary title of "sovereign prince" was given to the von Thurn und Taxis dynasty in the seventeenth century.

Gloria, who became Johannes's wife in 1980 and has since become the mother of his three children, could hardly have expected to be a serene highness and mistress of such a lavish estate, but, in many ways, she was an ideal match for her husband.

Her mother was a Hungarian noblewoman and her father could trace his family line back to the princes of the Holy Roman Empire. Born in Stuttgart, Germany, in 1960, she was christened Countess Mariae Gloria Ferdinanda Joachima Josephine Wilhelmine Huberta von Schoenburg-Glauchau.

The royal ancestry did not mean that the little countess grew up with the privileges enjoyed by the rich. Her father's people had lost their property, and for many years Gloria's family moved frequently as he looked for work as a journalist. They lived in Africa for five years before they settled in Munich. Despite this middle-class upbringing, Gloria was still a countess, a distant cousin, in fact, to Prince Johannes von Thurn und Taxis, and thus one of the very few women suitable to be his wife.

Johannes, thirty-four years older than Gloria, spent most of his adult life alone. He had gotten the reputation of being "the rebel prince" since he seemed to need no one, least of all a wife, to share his world. Johannes had powerful reasons for ending his bachelorhood, however. Family tradition required that in order to inherit the full fortune, he had to marry a member of another Roman Catholic princely house, and he had to produce a male heir from this marriage before his father's death. He found a wife and their son, Prince Albert, was born two months before the death of Johannes's father, Prince Karl Albert.

Although the bare facts might describe theirs as a "marriage of convenience," based more on their matched background then romance, Gloria and Johannes live very happily together. People who know the couple claim that it's more love than money that's behind their union.

The courtship of Gloria and Johannes was extravagant and romantic, far different from the arranged marriages of generations ago. They had met each other at various weddings and funerals of European royalty, but their first conversation was over coffee at a Munich café near the university where Gloria, then nineteen, was taking classes. They were attracted to each other; both had a keen sense of humor, and neither could tolerate dullness.

After three weeks of lunches and dinners, Johannes asked her to go with him to South America, a place that the prince loved intensely. Gloria, who was considering a shift to acting school at the time, accepted Johannes's offer on a whim, and she traveled with him to Brazil and then to St. Moritz in Switzerland. She now calls this decision (eventually choosing romance over college), "the right one," adding, "I wouldn't tell that to my children."[1]

The love affair flourished, despite the difference in their ages. "We only knew each other three months, and everybody knew we had found each other,"[2] she recalls.

Their wedding, on May 31, 1980, was held at the Palace of Regensburg, a 500-room castle brimming with antiques and priceless objects. The event brought all of international society to this small Bavarian city near Czechoslovakia. It was the grandest of parties, with Gloria in a designer gown topped by the diamond crown that was once owned by Marie Antoinette, the French queen who was beheaded during the French Revolution.

What the German aristocracy soon found out was that young Princess Gloria was not about to be quiet and shy in her new role. Although she was now a woman in charge of a vast dominion, she was determined to bring as much youthful energy into the palace as she could.

Her first challenge was to make the imposing structure at Regensburg a home. "You cannot imagine the stiffness and coldness that was here. I realized that right away, and I tried my best to make people feel a bit more cozy or nice."[3] Johannes, a clever man, did not expect her to become "queenly" or to act any older than she felt. "He always made me feel that everything stayed the same: You are still a young girl, and you have to keep natural,"[4] she said.

The prince and princess wanted to have a family immediately, not only because of the inheritance issue, but because they felt that children would enrich their lives more than the rooms full of possessions. Princess Maria Theresia was born in 1981, Princess Elisabeth in 1982, and in 1983, Prince Albert—an heir, at last—made his triumphant debut.

Raising a family is a responsibility that Gloria savors, and motherhood fits quite well into her unique view of being a liberated woman. On the one hand, she talks very traditionally, stating that duty to family comes first in her life. "I am very interested in politics, but I say a woman has to do politics in her house first. You have to see that your husband and your children are happy, and then you can do foreign policy."[5]

Although she would be overjoyed if her daughters were to marry princes, she insists that their happiness will be the key element in their marriage decisions. But Princess Gloria is not a traditionalist when it comes to enjoying all the experiences fate has granted her. The Thurn and Taxis royals may not have careers in the usual sense, but their globe-trotting schedule is demanding. They spend six months of the year in Regensburg and visit their five other castles in Germany. Each winter they spend two months in Brazil, where Prince Johannes owns a vast amount of land. In February, they're likely to be skiing in St. Moritz, and in October, they come to New York. Throughout the year, they go to Paris, London, and Munich and catch the sun on the Mediterranean.

Understandably, they have friends all over the world, and they like to socialize with many different types of people. They attend parties with other European royals—flying to have lunch at Kensington Palace with Prince Charles and Princess Diana isn't unusual. Business dinners are also common, since Johannes has managed to triple the family's fortune through wise financial investments.

More to Gloria's liking, however, are the parties she throws for her favorite artists and musicians. At these events, she can wear her wildest outfits (including the tall "witches' hats" that have become her trademark,) and her punk hairstyles that shimmer with real diamonds. She's interested in rock music and mixes easily with stars like Mick Jagger. She even persuaded Prince (the singer, not the husband) to perform at a Munich nightclub in order to raise money for a hospital devoted to helping burn patients—a clinic that the family helps support.

The stately rooms of Regensburg have vibrated with the music of young jazz musicians brought in to play at the Palace, and Gloria has staged contemporary plays in the gilded parlors.

While many a royal can be a patron of the arts, Gloria isn't content with merely applauding politely. She likes to participate. Dressed in studded leather, Gloria has made the chandeliers shake with her electric guitar playing. With no embarrassment, she went once to a local bar in New York City and belted out songs on the piano. She's updated the halls of Regensburg with displays of modern paintings and sculptures.

Another sign of Princess Gloria's sense of individuality is her approach to fashion. She enjoys being noticed, and therefore wears clothes that attract attention. Her towering hats and long capes, which used to be part of her wardrobe, made her look like a character out of a storybook—but certainly not like the fairly-tale princess. Now, her preference is for dresses with a poofy style. She follows fashion trends closely by attending fashion shows in Paris and New York, but she's known for finding one style and making it her own—without regard for whether it's "in" or "out."

Her jewelry collection, in contrast to the modish clothes, is strictly traditional. Most of her jewels are heirlooms from the Thurn und Taxis treasure chest, all extraordinary gems that couldn't be priced. And, since there is no point in being understated, according to Gloria's way of thinking, she wears the necklaces and bracelets and tiaras, rather than keeping them in a vault. They look all the more spectacular, however, because the princess sometimes wears no makeup and her hair is often cut like a boy's—short and simple. This contrast makes her bright dark eyes and impish smile shine as bright as the sapphires she wears.

With all the jewels she owns, she says that she's not attached to these ornaments. "I always call it 'the business thing' because I have to put it on for official things, but I don't need it."[6]

She is very proud of the estate that is Regensburg. Once a Medieval monastery, the palace is filled with antique fixtures, furniture, paintings, and porcelains. To illustrate the size of the building: the palace has so many antique clocks that one man must work full time just to keep them all wound. There are miles and miles of galleries, a library with 200,000 rare books, a 100-foot-long (30 m) nursery hall overflowing with toys and games, a hall of armaments, a hall of mirrors that's all gold and glass, and a throne room, in case a king or queen should pay a visit. The estate also includes a coach museum and a private chapel for the family, as well as a covered swimming pool and a bowling alley.

Gloria has made an effort to learn about the history behind each room, and visitors can get a three-hour tour from the princess that will cover about one-third of the interior.

Maintaining Regensburg is "a cross between running a hotel and a museum,"[7] Prince Johannes says. Gloria, who admits to being only mildly interested in decorating, is leaving the job of home maintenance and improvement to the experts.

In the summer, the couple enjoys spending time at the less formal Schloss Taxis, located in a deer-hunting forest. Consisting of four separate buildings, Schloss Taxis has been compared to a fairy tale castle, and it is more welcoming and less regal than Regensburg. Hunting parties are commonplace. In the coach house on the property, Gloria keeps her favorite royal coaches: classic American cars from the 1950s. She has seven models—coupes and convertibles with big fenders, lots of chrome, and wide, wide whitewall tires.

Gloria has another passion on the road. She loves to zip around the countryside on a motorbike. At first, the sight of their famous princess flying down the side streets stunned the local residents, who probably didn't understand why a woman who could be chauffeured would want to do such a thing. "I had such a tough time making people understand that I need it just to go once a week in the summer for a ride somewhere, and to be just a normal somebody else."[8]

Considering the lavish lifestyle the prince and princess lead, some might wonder whether they are resented for their wealth. In Germany, and in Regensburg particularly, the family is highly respected for its contributions to charity. Gloria, in her own dramatic way, has raised money through parties and performances; she has even tried to help the mentally ill patients in the town's asylum by getting these people to act in play productions she's staged.

Princess Gloria may have interrupted her formal education when she met Johannes, but she has begun her studies again. Professors from the University of Regensburg visit the palace and teach her history, economics, and theology. Medicine is another area that fascinates her, and she is absorbing a knowledge of architecture through lessons from those who maintain the palace.

Religion is not merely a course of study for Princess Gloria. She considers herself very religious and says she wants to know more about her Roman Catholic faith and other religions. In keeping with her independent attitude, though, she doesn't believe in a strict set of religious do's and don'ts. "It's not important to follow the rules, and if you follow the rules and do bad things, it's even worse. Don't follow the rules, but be a good person and thank God for what you have—that's my philosophy."[9]

With three lovely children, a husband who appreciates her off-beat approach to life, and a personality that adds sizzle to society, it seems that Princess Gloria von Thurn und Taxis has much to be thankful for. Could she exist as happily without the palaces and servants and the designer clothes? She thinks so.

"I didn't live on a large budget before I married. And I enjoy life so much. I'm not attached to material things."[10] Gloria is also truthful enough to add: "But if you ask me this question thirty years from now, I'm not sure I would say yes. Because you get used to wealth, you get used to good living, very, very quickly."[11] Rich or not, royal or not, she says, "the most important thing in life is to be happy with what you have."[12]

## CATHERINE OXENBERG

Palaces, movie studios, ski resorts, and a million-aire's villa in Spain—these would be the sets for Catherine Oxenberg's life if ever a film was made about this young American actress with royal blood.

Her background is a study in contrasts and co-incidences. Her mother is H.R.H. Princess Eliza-beth of Yugoslavia, whose family lost the crown when Elizabeth was very young, but who remains very much a royal. Her father is Howard Oxen-berg, a New York City clothing tycoon and, de-spite his wealth, very much a commoner.

Because of this heritage, Catherine Oxenberg is not a princess herself, yet her upbringing was one of privilege. She has socialized with the best royal families of Europe and she's played the part of a princess several times in television dramas, winning the roles, her directors say, because of her classy, cool beauty—a characteristic people associate with royalty.

In her first television appearance, Catherine played Lady Diana in a movie that told the story of the British royal romance. Oxenberg proved to be an excellent choice for the production since she had actually met Diana at the royal ball following the couple's wedding and had known the Prince, a relative, since her youth. In the TV series "Dynasty," she acted as the spoiled daughter of Alexis and Blake Carrington, later to become, at least on screen, the bride of Prince Michael of Moldavia.

With no royal title of her own, Catherine Oxenberg doesn't pretend to be a princess. She has said many times that she'd find true royal life too confining. "I think in many ways, being a princess is an obstacle and a hindrance. People look at you as a dodo bird, a strange, obsolete creature who's not quite real."[1]

Like her sister, Christina, who's two years younger and quite successful as an author, Catherine was brought up with many of the advantages that royal children enjoy. She lived in Europe as well as America, accompanying her mother on vacations around the world and meeting important people. Yet she has also developed all-American tastes—she loves deli sandwiches, fitness classes, and, most of all, the Hollywood dream.

Catherine was born in New York in 1961, the year after her parents were married. Princess Elizabeth and Howard Oxenberg were an unlikely couple. Princess Elizabeth was supposed to marry the king of the Belgians when she met Oxenberg on a ski slope. Against her parents' wishes, she eloped with the handsome American businessman four days after they had met.

Catherine and her sister were born in America. When Catherine was three, however, her parents divorced, and she went to London with her mother.

As a child, Catherine was a loner, partly because of the family's frequent moves. She didn't have the chance to make close friendships. When Catherine was thirteen, her mother was engaged for a brief time to Richard Burton, the great British actor. Burton was famous for his brilliant acting, his two marriages to Elizabeth Taylor, and his heavy drinking. But to Catherine, he was an early mentor, someone who taught her and took her seriously. Burton made a lasting impression on the young girl's life, although he and Catherine's mother were together for only a year.

"He sparked the fantasy of acting,"[2] she says. She saw in him a man who was fiercely intelligent and inquisitive—a role model. During this time, he coached her in Shakespearean sonnets for her school productions; they did crossword puzzles for hours. He also taught her how to drive, propping her up on six pillows so she could see over the steering wheel.

Ambitious and smart, Catherine now knew the path she wanted to take. During a Christmas vacation with her father in New York, she decided that she should live in the United States. The announcement made her mother furious, but Catherine had the support of her father and, more importantly, was determined to make the choice for herself.

As it turned out, Catherine did not have an easy time of it as an American high school student. Her new classmates at St. Paul's School mocked her English accent. Despite not fitting in, she graduated with top honors and was accepted by Harvard University.

At this juncture of her life, Catherine made another decision that stunned her family. Scratching plans to go to Harvard, she moved to New York City to break into modeling and continued her education through night-school courses at Columbia University.

Since she's only five feet, six inches (169 cm) tall, Catherine was considered by some modeling agencies to be too short for the job. She was persistent, though. A bright new face, with perfect bones, is hard for magazines to ignore for long, and her big break as a model came very quickly; *Vogue* magazine used her for a ten-page fashion spread.

Catherine's strong desire to become an actress, together with a stroke of good luck, led to another big break. Her mother had encouraged her to take acting classes and get an agent who would watch for possible roles. In 1982, on only her second audition, she was chosen for a special assignment. With no screen-acting experience, Catherine was given the part of Lady Diana in the TV movie "The Royal Romance of Charles and Diana."

Catherine certainly had the physical features to play the part; she and Diana have a similar soft, blond prettiness. The natural English accent was another plus in the American actress's favor, as was her look of innocence.

What Catherine didn't realize was that her royal credits would come under criticism. First, the British royal circles objected to the television production. The family felt it might be demeaning. Catherine's mother solved this problem by sending Prince Charles a copy of the script, and he responded, saying that if such a movie had to be made, he was pleased that Catherine could, at least, bring some dignity to it.

With these relations smoothed over, Catherine then had to face the American critics, who charged that she won the part because of her royal connections. This was not true, since the producers did not even know of her family background until halfway through the shooting.

The episode was upsetting, but Catherine said she learned a valuable lesson from the outcry—the importance of having a "thick skin," and not letting other people's opinions affect you.

After filming the special, Catherine did a little more modeling, yet her heart and mind were elsewhere—in Spain. She had met Manuel de Prado, a rich Spanish banker, and he asked her to marry him. She moved to Madrid, where for nearly two years, she was his fiancée and lived as the lady of the manor, trying to fit into Manuel's lifestyle. She learned Spanish and rode horses (he was a polo player), but there was little chance for her to pursue her career in this setting. Catherine reluctantly returned to the

United States in 1983, claiming that she wasn't ready to give up her professional goals. She ended her relationship, although she said she still loved the Spanish millionaire.

She moved back to New York City for a few weeks and then flew to Los Angeles with the hope that Hollywood would give her another chance to prove her talents as an actress. She's always been spontaneous in making major decisions, she says. "Whenever you have the courage to let go of a situation that you're not happy with, you are invariably rewarded."[3]

Oxenberg's timing was perfect. After three months on the West Coast, meeting the "right" people, she was called to audition for a new role on the television program "Dynasty." To cast the part of Amanda Carrington, the producers had seen about 200 young women, had tested a dozen, and finally decided that Catherine Oxenberg was their top choice. Catherine was twenty-two years old and possessed the sophistication and innocence that made her ideal for the part.

Joining a group of actors as a "new character" can be difficult. On screen, the "Dynasty" clan, after all, carries on like royalty with their spats and extravagant ways. But it only took Catherine a few weeks to discover her on-screen personality, and to be accepted by the other members of the cast.

The acting challenge appealed to Catherine, especially because the Amanda Carrington role had more vinegar than sugar. Catherine had to be believable as the daughter of Alexis (played by Joan

Collins), a ruthless woman who schemed for power. She was relieved not to be locked into the delicate princess image following the Diana role. "It's such wonderful work getting paid instead to be horrible,"[4] she commented.

For the sake of the show, the characters of Alexis and Amanda had to be competitive with each other. On the "Dynasty" set, however, Collins and Oxenberg were chummy, with the star often giving the starlet tips on how to command a scene.

When acting in a weekly television series, a high energy level is a necessity. After her first year on the show, Catherine felt the strain of long hours in the studio and on location. Her schedule was to get up at 5 A.M., rush to the studio, sit quietly during makeup and hair styling, be ready on the set, and then wait until her scene was shot. The days stretched until 7 or 8 P.M., and she had to be in bed by 10 P.M. in order to be "up" for the next day's work.

Although she had always believed in the value of keeping fit, Catherine learned how to pace herself and began working with a physical fitness trainer, who came to her rented Beverly Hills house three times a week. "I'm too lazy to go to the gym,"[5] she admitted. Skiing and tennis are two sports she excels in, and like the character she played on television, Catherine is competitive. Winning—or at least doing one's best—is the key to enjoying a game.

When asked to compare herself to her "Dynasty" character, Catherine offered this thought: "Amanda is bright, and she has a sense of humor and she is very strong-willed, as I am. She's not a coward and neither am I."[6] Catherine also considered herself more mature than Amanda and less aggressive when it came to meeting men.

The pressure of show business can be hard on young women, but Catherine's self-confidence is one of her greatest assets. She doesn't run away from a difficult situation. She was, nevertheless, terrified when she was asked to host the "Saturday Night Live" television show. It meant that she had to experience a whole series of firsts—she had to perform in front of a live audience for the first time, do comedy for the first time, and speak with a variety of accents.

The opportunity came about by sheer chance and was another instance of Catherine being in the right place at the right time. An associate producer recognized her while the two were sitting in a New York City coffee shop. The show needed a host at the last minute and here was this TV actress. Hired on a Tuesday night, she rehearsed nonstop until the Saturday performance, coming through the ordeal with flying colors. "You feel horror, but when you're up there for two minutes and suddenly you get a response, it gets to the point where you feel that what you're talking to is alive. Suddenly the adrenaline rush hits and it's just the biggest thrill, the biggest high."[7]

Her "Dynasty" experience came to an end when her contract was not renewed. Catherine reluctantly returned to modeling while auditioning for other parts. In 1987, she landed a role that she was destined to play—the young princess longing for adventure in the television movie "Roman Holiday."

In real life, Catherine has remained unmarried and uncommitted since her romance with the Spanish banker. She has dated Prince Albert of Monaco, and this has been the subject of many rumors. Most of her social life centers around the West Coast, where the acting jobs are, and where she lives with her two cats Tristan and Isolde, named after classical lovers.

Her mother, the princess, has never urged Catherine to marry a member of royalty, since Elizabeth felt the sting of her parents' disapproval of her own marriage. The two women have a close relationship. They attend parties together, spend holidays together, and vacation together. "She is more like a sister to me,"[8] Catherine has said. Mother and daughter also have posed together for cosmetics advertisements.

Like most young women who are trying hard to succeed, Catherine has moments when she is insecure, doubting her abilities to make it in a profession that is brimming with determined and beautiful women. At times, she wonders whether she'll land another part, she says, while quickly insisting that acting is something she must do. "Acting is the only art form I feel capable of using to express myself. I feel comfortable in front of the camera."[9]

Her goal, amidst the fantasies and false hopes of Hollywood, is to remain true to herself. "I'm not impressed with people for the wrong reasons. I'll never take myself too seriously, and I'll never believe all the stuff they write about me."[10]

For the actress and the almost-princess, these are wise words.

# CONCLUSION

Anyone who probes the lives of young royals realizes that being a princess holds many meanings. There are, first of all, several ways one can become "Her Royal Highness." A princess can be born of royal blood as a direct descendant of a king or queen. The birth is heralded by much celebration within the country and the little girl is raised with the understanding that as a royal, she must serve her nation for her entire life. Princess Martha Louise of Norway, Princesses Caroline and Stephanie of Monaco, and the two princesses of Spain all have held their titles since birth. They learned to wave to the crowd from the time they were little.

There are also those women who instantly became princesses when they married a prince. Lady Diana received her title, Princess of Wales, in such a fashion, and Princess Gloria von Thurn und Taxis, who had been a countess, gained her princess status when she wed a sovereign prince. For these young women, there were lessons to learn in the process. Diana was instructed how to walk, talk, sit, and eat with regal grace, while Gloria, who possesses an explosive personality, has had to learn about the family heritage in order to give palace guests an indepth tour through the museumlike halls of her vast estate.

In this book, chapters were included on several women who do not have the official title, yet have the royal connection that identifies them as princesses. American actress Catherine Oxenberg, for instance, is the daughter of Princess Elizabeth of Yugoslavia and an American businessman, so she is a commoner with a royal background. Sarah Ferguson, the wife of Prince Andrew, had no title of nobility until she married; she is now the Duchess of York, yet is still known as "Fergie."

Not all of the modern princesses have a kingdom. Princess Elizabeth of Toro works as an ambassador for her country, Uganda, but is not accorded special royal standing in the nation since it is no longer a monarchy. And Princess Yasmin Aga Khan, the granddaughter of the cultural leader of the Islamic people, has no dominion. In the democratic state of Germany, Princess Gloria von Thurn und Taxis credits her royal standing to the hereditary title that was given her husband's dynasty long ago. In this case, the family became royalty because of its extensive land holdings.

Countries that are monarchies depend on their royal families to serve as national symbols, to be enthusiastic goodwill representatives so that elected political leaders can concentrate their efforts on the government's legislation and administration. In most monarchies, therefore, the royals have little, if any, power to make decisions affecting social changes, and this makes the royal family's work largely ceremonial. They are "figureheads," respected for their role but with little political power.

In other countries, such as Spain and, to some extent, the Principality of Monaco, royalty plays a more important part in determining the laws of the land.

A total of ten European countries maintain their monarchies. But there are kings and queens in other parts of the world, as well. Among those royals not as well known: Princess Sayako, the daughter of Japan's new emperor; the three royal princesses of Thailand; the many female descendants of the King of Saudi Arabia, and Princess Constance Christina, the teenage daughter of the ruler of Lesotho in Africa.

However limited the political power of these royal leaders, the country's first family is expected to fulfill the duties as titular head of the state, and to serve with grace and dignity.

For adult princesses, this regimen involves a full-time schedule of making appearances at public gatherings and serving as official hostesses at important functions. Princesses with hereditary titles and no official state responsibilities, such as Princess Elizabeth of Toro, are not supported by the country and thus can work in whatever area appeals to them. And some princesses can attempt to have their cake and eat it too—to juggle their royal obligations with careers far removed from the palace. Princess Stephanie, for example, has started a swimsuit design business and recorded rock albums while still continuing to play her official role in Monaco.

Despite differences in the scope of their responsibilities, there are many shared characteristics common to royal princesses everywhere. To be realistic, we must admit that these young women aren't necessarily beautiful or exceptionally intelligent, but they are necessarily rich. If a country has a monarchy, a percentage of the citizens' taxes is spent to support the royal family. Most ordinary folk like the concept of having blueblooded members of their society as representative of the best, most cultured people in the country. Consequently, royal homes are usually large and lavish palaces, furnished with antiques and priceless paintings. The family's closets are filled with designer clothes, regal garments, and family jewels. Its vacations are spent in the most glamorous places, and there are often many servants to make this life-style possible.

Yet, while modern-day princesses never need to worry about making ends meet, most recognize that they have a duty to contribute to society. They help raise money for social causes, such as aiding underprivileged people, supporting the arts, or leading the fight against disease.

Members of royalty are expected to give their energy in exchange for the special treatment they're accorded. Princess Caroline of Monaco is active in many organizations, notably the Princess Grace Foundation, an institution named for her mother that has brought ballet to the tiny principality. Princess Sayako of Japan, not yet twenty years old, is interested in programs that train guide dogs for the blind. And, in what might be the most unselfish illustration of dedication, Princess Yasmin Aga Khan has devoted her adult years to raising money in the battle against Alzheimer's disease, the mental disorder that took the life of her mother.

The royals of Great Britain make frequent appearances on behalf of various social causes. Buckingham Palace posts the daily schedules of Princess Diana and the Duchess of York so that the press can report on their visits to hospitals and fundraisers, which further publicizes these good works. Even Princess Gloria has labored for charity, bringing her rock musician friends to a little German town in order to raise money for its burn clinic.

The royal timetable might sound like shaking hands during the day and attending lavish parties at night, and viewed that way, the ceremonial duties of princesses don't seem that different from what their ancestors used to do. The royal standard has changed tremendously, though, in terms of what a princess is permitted to do beyond her ceremonial duties.

Unlike their predecessors, contemporary princesses are eager for formal education. Instead of being tutored at the palace, they attend classes locally. Many of them go to public schools. A university education is not unusual for a princess anymore, and after graduation, if they are energetic and independent in spirit, the royals can work in the community.

Princess Elena of Spain teaches at an elementary school in Madrid; Belgium's Princess Marie-Esmeralda is a journalist in Paris; Princess Irene of Greece, the sister of the Queen of Spain, lives in London and tours as a concert pianist, and Princess Sophie of Romania works as a painter. In one of the most publicized career launches among royalty, Princess Stephanie already has proven herself in two different professions, an interesting fact considering that thirty years ago, Monaco society pushed her mother, the famous movie actress, to give up acting when she became Prince Rainier's wife.

Modern-day princesses have more responsibilities and more personal options in the ways they live their lives, but they also must deal with some long-standing traditions that limit their actions. Even in our more open times, today's royal princesses are not always allowed to act as they please, whether it be in choosing a husband or behaving in public. The code of behavior is strict, and royals have to be able to tolerate publicity since they are always in the public eye.

Although the concept of arranged marriages died out in most cultures during the last century, for royal families there is still an understanding that a prince or princess should choose a mate of the same social standing. In ancient times, the king or queen would decide on the acceptable suitors for their princess. Commoners were below consideration. The final choice would be made by the parents, and the royal union would often depend on international politics. If the ruler wanted to improve relations or avoid war with another country, he might marry off his daughter to a prince of a strategic region. The personal happiness of the two was never the issue.

Only in the past twenty to thirty years have the barriers for royal marriage broken down. The present crown prince of Norway managed to marry a commoner, although it took nine years of government debate before the wedding was allowed to take place. Since then, there have been other marriages that have united a royal with a nonroyal. Parents still hope, though, that their royal princess will find her true love among the titled aristocrats, so that the royal lineage can continue smoothly and without question.

Princess Elizabeth of Yugoslavia defied her parents by marrying a commoner, and her children, Catherine and Christina Oxenberg, have no official royal status. And, although Queen Sofia of Spain says that she will accept her daughters' decisions on marriage (the king does not have to grant approval), the royal pair has been thorough in introducing their daughters to the eligible royals in a manner similar to the way the king and queen first got to know each other when they were young.

Restrictions don't only pertain to marriage. Princess Elena of Spain may not live outside the country until her younger brother, the crown prince, has married and had a male heir. This constraint makes it doubly difficult for the princess to become seriously involved with anyone, since the man has to have royal ties and be willing to live in Spain.

Royal observers could argue that the rules for marriage are much more relaxed than ever before. In 1978, Princess Caroline of Monaco not only married a commoner, she did so against the wishes of her family. Two years later, she filed for a legal divorce and, while the royal circles shook a little from this wrenching event, it did not stop Caroline from becoming a much-admired member of royalty now that she's happy in her second marriage.

With their every movement analyzed by high society and the general public, princesses are expected to behave differently from the average young woman. And a princess, more so than a prince, has to conform, to act properly at all times. She has to dress elegantly—but not too stylishly—and carry herself in such a manner that there is never a hint of tiredness, boredom, silliness, anger, or disappointment showing in her face. To be sure, shouting—even for joy—is out, according to royal tradition.

The pressure of having to be perfect can be a strain, particularly when news magazines and television cameras record every minor comment and action made by the royals. If the teenage princess has a new boyfriend, the news is publicized around the world. If a young royal mother wants to play with her children on the beach, there are photographers crowding her (or hiding in the bushes) in order to get the shots. In this respect, a princess's life is made much more trying because she must be patient with invasions of her privacy.

Amidst the privileges that are granted to them, princesses in these modern times struggle to strike a balance between state responsibility and personal freedom. Attached to the past by their heritage, the contemporary royals are nevertheless eager for a more modern role to play, and they are setting new standards for independence—not through earning money, because they're already financially secure—but by using their time and talents in ways to make their countries better.

When we read about their worlds, we find that a princess is not a stiff, make-believe character. She is, rather, more capable than her ancestors could ever imagine. What's more, she is quite real and ordinary in trying to cope with a life filled with duties, problems, fun, heartaches, accomplishments, and love.

# SOURCE NOTES

## PRINCESS CAROLINE

1. "Monaco's Reigning Beauty," *McCall's,* September 1986.
2. "Royal Intrigue: Will Caroline Snatch the Throne from Her Brother Albert?," *Good Housekeeping,* June 1988.
3. "Princess Caroline Takes Charge," *European Travel & Life,* April 1988.
4. "Monaco's Reigning Beauty," *McCall's,* September 1986.
5. Ibid.
6. "Princess Caroline Takes Charge," *European Travel & Life,* April 1988.

## PRINCESS STEPHANIE

1. "Royal Intrigue: Will Caroline Snatch the Throne from her Brother Albert?," *Good Housekeeping,* June 1988.
2. Ibid.
3. "Pop Goes the Princess," *Us,* Feb. 9, 1987.
4. "Thanks to a Curious Family Friend, Princess Stephanie's in the Swim—and Daddy's in Deep Water." *People,* September 30, 1985.
5. "Monaco Lands Hollywood, the Second Time Around," *People,* March 1, 1987.

6. "Pop Goes the Princess," *Us,* Feb. 9, 1987.
7. Ibid.
8. "Hey Prince Rainier, Guess Who's Coming to the Palace?," *People,* March 17, 1987.
9. "Pop Goes the Princess," *Us,* Feb. 9, 1987.
10. Ibid.
11. Ibid.
12. Ibid.
13. Ibid.

## PRINCESS ELIZABETH OF TORO

1. CBS News Interview, "Sixty Minutes," February 7, 1988.
3. Ibid.
3. Ibid.
4. Ibid.
5. "Actress, Model, Lawyer, Diplomat," *New York Times,* December 21, 1986.
6. "Talking to . . . Elizabeth of Toro," *Vogue,* February 1988.
7. CBS News Interview, "Sixty Minutes," February 7, 1988.

## PRINCESS YASMIN AGA KHAN

1. "My Mother, Rita Hayworth," *McCall's,* May 1987.
2. Ibid.
3. Ibid.
4. Ibid.
5. Ibid.
6. Ibid.
7. Ibid.
8. Ibid.
9. Ibid.
10. Ibid.

## PRINCESS DIANA

1. "Di on Di," *People,* Spring 1988.
2. "The Lady Who Would Be Queen," *People,* Spring 1988.
3. Josephine Fairley, *The Princess and the Duchess* (New York: St. Martin's, 1989).
4. "The Lady Who Would be Queen," *People,* Spring 1988.
5. "Around the Clock," *People,* Spring 1988.
6. "Di on Di," *People,* Spring 1988.
7. "Diana's Life as Wife, Mother, and Princess," *Good Housekeeping,* June 1983.

## SARAH FERGUSON

1. Josephine Fairley, *The Princess and the Duchess* (New York: St. Martin's, 1989).
2. Ibid.
3. "Fergie's Life Story," *Good Housekeeping,* July 1988.
4. "Fabulous Fergie Riding High," *Ladies Home Journal,* Feb. 1987.
5. "Fergie's Life Story," *Good Housekeeping,* July 1988.
6. Ibid.
7. Ibid.
8. Ibid.
9. Ibid.
10. Josephine Fairley, *The Princess and the Duchess* (New York: St. Martins, 1989).
11. "Fergie's Life Story," *Good Housekeeping,* July 1988.


## PRINCESS GLORIA

1. "The Dynamite Socialite, Princess TNT of Bavaria," *Vanity Fair,* September 1985.
2. Ibid.
3. Ibid.
4. Ibid.
5. Ibid.
6. Ibid.
7. "The Riches of Regensburg," *Architectural Digest,* January 1985.
8. "The Dynamite Socialite, Princess TNT of Bavaria," *Vanity Fair,* September 1985.
9. Ibid.
10. Ibid.
11. Ibid.
12. Ibid.


## CATHERINE OXENBERG

1. "Princess Charming," *McCall's,* May 1986.
2. Ibid.
3. "Catherine Oxenberg," *Interview,* July 1986.
4. "Mother is a Princess . . . Father Had Four Wives . . . Then There Was the Titled Spaniard," *TV Guide,* June 5, 1985.
5. "Princess Charming," *McCall's,* May 1986.
6. Ibid.
7. "Catherine Oxenberg," *Interview,* July 1986.
8. "Mother is a Princess . . ." *TV Guide,* June 5, 1985.
9. Ibid.
10. "Princess Charming," *McCall's,* May 1986.

# FOR FURTHER
# READING

*Books*

Ashdown, Dulcie M. *Royal Children*. London: Hale, 1979.

Ashraf, Princess of Iran. *Faces in a Mirror: Memoirs from Exile*. Englewood Cliffs, N.J.: Prentice-Hall, 1980.

Bennet, Daphne. *Queen Victoria's Children*. London: V. Gollancz, 1980.

Boulay de la Meurthe, Laure. *There Are Still Kings: The Ten Royal Families of Europe*. New York: C. N. Potter, 1984.

Cathcart, Helen. *Anne and the Princesses Royal*. London, New York: W. H. Allen, 1973.

Courtney, Nicholas. *Royal Children*. London: J. H. Dent, 1982.

Fox, Mary V. *Princess Diana*. New Jersey: Enslow Pubs., 1986.

Gibson, Peter. *The Concise Guide to Kings and Queens: A Thousand Years Of European Monarchy*. Exeter, England: Hebb & Bower, 1985.

Green, Carol. *Diana, Princess of Wales*. Chicago: Children's, 1985.

Kidd, Charles. *Debrett's Book of Royal Children*. London: J. M. Dent, 1982.

Michael, Princess of Kent. *Crowned in a Far Country: Portraits of Eight Royal Brides*. London: Weidenfeld & Nicolson, 1986.

Ross, Josephine. *The Winter Queen: The Story of Elizabeth Stuart*. London: Weidenfeld and Nicolson, 1979.

Turner, Dorothy. *Queen Elizabeth I*. New York: Franklin Watts, 1987.

Wallace, Ann. *Royal Mothers: From Eleanor of Aquitaine to Princess Diana*. London: Piatkus, 1987.

White-Thompson, Stephen. *Elizabeth I & Tudor England*. New York: Franklin Watts, 1985.

*Magazines*

"Dynasties." *National Review,* November 28, 1980.

"Europe's Most Eligible Royal Catches," *Town & Country,* April 1986.

"How Europe Treats Its Other Royal Families." *U.S. News & World Report,* August 3, 1981.

"Real-life Royals: Which One Could Be Right For You?" *Teen,* October 1985.

"The Year of the Royal Mess." *Good Housekeeping,* November 1987.

# BIBLIOGRAPHY

## PRINCESS CAROLINE

*Books*
Bradford, Sarah. *Princess Grace*. New York: Stein and Day, 1984.
Hassy, Christian de, Baron. *Palace: My Life in the Royal Family of Monaco*. New York: Atheneum, 1986.
Spada, James. *Grace: the Secret Lives of a Princess*. Garden City, N.Y.: Doubleday, 1987.

*Magazines*
Barrett, Katherine. "The Legacy of Princess Grace," *Ladies Home Journal,* April 1983.
Crimp, Susan, and Patricia Burstein. "Will Caroline Snatch the Throne of Monaco from her Brother Albert?," *Good Housekeeping,* June 1988.
Di liberto, Gioia. "A New Beginning for Monaco's Princess," *People,* June 25, 1984.
De Dubovay, Diane, "Monaco's Reigning Beauty," *McCall's,* September 1986.
"How Her Baby Has Changed Princess Caroline—and Monaco." *Good Housekeeping,* January 1985.
Fayard, Judy. "A Job Fit for a Princess," *Life,* April 1986.
"Princess Caroline: a Legacy of Duty, Obedience . . . and Guilt," *People,* April 25, 1988.

"Princess Caroline is Content in Charlotte's Web, Despite Rumors of a Troubled Marriage," *People,* August 18, 1986.

Stratte-McClure, Joel. "Princess Caroline Takes Charge," *European Travel & Life,* April 1988.


## PRINCESS STEPHANIE

*Books*

Bradford, Sarah. *Princess Grace.* New York: Stein and Day, 1984.

Hassy, Christian de, Baron. *Palace: My Life in the Royal Family of Monaco.* New York: Atheneum, 1986.

Spada, James. *Grace: the Secret Lives of a Princess.* Garden City, N.Y.: Doubleday, 1987.


*Magazines*

Aitken, Lee. "Monaco and Hollywood, the Second Time Around," *People,* March 10, 1986.

Di liberto, Gioia. "High Intrigue and Haute Couture: the Tainted Troubled Times of Monaco's Princess Stephanie," *People,* November 19, 1984.

"Hey Prince Rainier, Guess Who's Coming to the Palace," *People,* March 17, 1987.

Laing, Roger, and Cathy Nolan. "Belmondo or Delon? Monaco's Racy Princess Stephanie Makes Waves with a New Beau," *People,* August 27, 1984.

"Princess Stephanie: Her Model's Portfolio," *People,* April 15, 1985.

"Rock and Roll Royalty," *Elle,* December 1986.

"Thanks to a Curious 'Family Friend,' Princess Stephanie's in the Swim—and Daddy's in Deep Water," *People,* September 30, 1985.


## PRINCESS ELIZABETH
## OF TORO

*Books*

Elizabeth, Princess of Toro. *African Princess: the Story of Princess Elizabeth of Toro.* London: Hamilton, 1987.

*Magazines and Newspapers*

Booker, Simeon. "African Princess Survives Scandal, Becomes Diplomat," *Jet,* June 30, 1986.

Gamarekian, Barbara. "Actress, Lawyer, Model, Diplomat," *New York Times,* December 21, 1986.

Maxa, Rudy. "Talking to . . . Elizabeth of Toro," *Vogue,* February 1988.

Reasoner, Harry. "Elizabeth of Toro," Sixty Minutes Transcripts, February 7, 1988.

## PRINCESS MARTHA LOUISE
## OF NORWAY

*Books*

Bjaaland, Patricia C. *The Norwegian Royal Family.* Oslo, Norway: TANO Als Publishing Co., 1986.

Faarlund, Thorbjorn, Ed., *Facts About Norway.* Oslo, Norway: Chr. Schibsted Forlag (publishers), 1987.


## PRINCESS DIANA

*Books*

*A Week in the life of the Royal Family.* by the staff of *The Sunday Express Magazine.* New York: Macmillan, 1983.

Darling, David J. *Diana, the People's Princess.* Minneapolis, Minn.: Dillon Press, 1984.

Fairley, Josephine. *The Princess and the Duchess.* New York: St. Martin's, 1989.

Junor, Penny. *Diana, Princess of Wales: A Biography.* Garden City, N.Y.: Doubleday, 1983.

Martin, Ralph G. *Charles & Diana.* New York: Putnam, 1985.

*Magazines*

Barry, Stephen. "Diana's Everyday Life as a Wife, Mother & Princess," *Good Housekeeping,* June 1983.

Bernstein, Fred, and Laura Ferguson. "Now Playing at the Palace . . . Fergie and Di, the Best of Friends and the Toast of the Town," *People,* October 13, 1986.

"Diana: a Celebration," *Ladies Home Journal,* July 1986.

Dillon, Sheila. "Good-bye, Shy Di!", *McCall's,* March 1985.

Holden, Anthony. "The Origin and Future of a Royal Marriage," *People,* July 1981.

Johnson, Bonnie. "Autumn of their Discontent," *People,* November 7, 1987.

Junor, Peggy. "Diana, the Lady Who Charmed a Prince," *Cosmopolitan,* June 1983.

Kaufman, Joanne. "Seven-year hitch: on its Seventh Anniversary, Charles and Diana's Marriage Suggests that Even Royalty Must Face Reality," *People,* August 1, 1988.

Keay, Douglas. "Solving the Puzzle of Diana's Marriage," *Good Housekeeping,* May 1988.

*People,* Spring 1988 Special Issue.

"Princess Diana," *People,* December 28, 1987.

Robyns, Gwen. "Diana: When a Princess Becomes a Superstar!", *Ladies Home Journal,* June 1983.

Schwartz, Alan. "It's Not Easy to Be a Princess," *Seventeen,* November 1984.

Seward, Ingrid. "The Di Look—And How to Get It," *Redbook,* October 1988.

Waugh, Denis, and Gail Ridgwell. "The Wedding of the Century: Getting Ready for the Big Day," *Life,* July 1981.

Weinhouse, Beth. "The Princess and her Protegé," *Ladies Home Journal,* July 1986.

Weinhouse, Beth, and Gwen Robyns. "The Princess Who Loves Children," *Ladies Home Journal,* July 1984.

## SARAH FERGUSON

*Books*

Fairley, Josephine. *The Princess and the Duchess.* New York: St. Martin's, 1989.

*Magazines*

"The Ascent of Sarah," *Life,* March 1988.

"Bye, Bye Baby," *People,* August 1, 1988.

"Fergie and Andy name their Baby Bea, and All Britain is Abuzz," *People,* September 5, 1988.

"Fergie Wins Her Wings and Andy's a Backseat Pilot," *People,* March 2, 1987.

Holder, Margaret. "Fergie: Can She Bring Up Her Baby—Her Way?", *Redbook,* August 1988.

Junor, Penny. "Will Motherhood Change Fergie?", *McCall's,* June 1988.

Kaufman, Joanne. "For Fergie, Mum's the Word," *People,* August 29, 1988.

Keay, Douglas. "A Baby for Fergie and Andrew," *Good Housekeeping,* May 1988.

Keay, Douglas. "Andrew and 'Fergie'—Royalty's Happiest Most Unusual Marriage," *Good Housekeeping,* April 1987.

"Little Veggie," *People,* September 26, 1988.

Pearson, Susie, and David Thomas. "All About Fergie: Her Flair, Her Flubs, and the Kind of Mother She'll Be," *Ladies Home Journal,* August 1988.

Robyns, Gwen. "Fabulous Fergie; Flying High," *Ladies Home Journal,* February 1987.

"Sarah, Duchess of York," *Current Biography,* March 1987.

Smith, Terry, and Laura Sanderson. "Fantastic Fergie," *People,* April 7, 1986.

"To Love, Honor—and Obey?", *Time,* July 21, 1986.

Wallace, Carol. "The Royal Wedding," *People,* August 4, 1986.

Whitaker, James. "A Triumphant Transformation: Fergie's First Year," *McCall's,* June 1987.

## PRINCESSES ELENA
## AND CRISTINA OF SPAIN

*Magazines*

Guppy, Shusha. "Sofia: Spain's Exemplary Queen," *Town & Country,* April 1988.

"A Visit with the King of Spain," *Life* December 1985.

"Spain Salutes an Heir Apparent," *People,* Feb 17, 1986.


## PRINCESS GLORIA
## VON THURN UND TAXIS

*Magazines*

Michael, Prince of Greece. "The Riches of Regensburg," *Architectural Digest,* January 1985.

Richardson, John III. "Rock 'n' Royalty," *House & Garden,* April 1988.

"The Dynamite Socialite, Princess TNT of Bavaria," *Vanity Fair,* September 1985.


## CATHERINE OXENBERG

*Magazines*

Price, Susan. "Mother Is a Princess . . . Father Had Four Wives . . . Then There Was the Titled Spaniard," *TV Guide,* June 15, 1985.

"Time Out Dressing," *Harper's Bazaar,* February 1985.

Yorkshire, Heidi. "Princess Charming," *McCall's,* May 1986.

Wallace, David. "Her Family Lost the Crown of Yugoslavia so Catherine Oxenberg Opts for a TV Dynasty," *People,* May 18, 1985.

# INDEX